John TJ Diggs

L♡VE L✝FE

Can You 👊 DIGG It?

Publisher Information

Print ISBN 978-1-73457-590-3

eBook 978-1-73457-591-0

Edited by E. Lee Caleca

A SYSTEM OF THOUGHT TO POWERFULLY CHANGE YOUR LIFE FOREVER!!!

INTRODUCTION

For millions of years, humans have asked a very powerful thought-provoking question: What is the purpose of life? Why are we here? Scholars, prophets, philosophers, poets, and paupers have all shared millions of possible answers to that question. What is the purpose of this thing called Life? In fact, there have been so many great possible answers, that today most people are still uncertain and unsettled about their own purpose. People are still asking the same question.

What am I doing here?

With that being said, and in honor of my divine mission to make a positive impact in the world, I would like to share with you what I believe to be the purpose of life. The purpose of my life, the purpose of your life, the purpose of our lives is simply to Love it!

Love Life!

The fundamental purpose of our lives is for us to apply our most powerful emotion, Love, to the experience of life itself.

Love Life! Can You DIGG It?

In short, the ultimate drive is to be in love with the experience of being alive; spiritual beings unconditionally in love with the human experience. And "unconditionally" means not only loving life when it's good to us, but loving life when it's not so good to us as well. You don't stop loving your kids when they misbehave or your spouse when he or she is annoying or frustrating. And it's the same with life. Love it despite its setbacks, challenges, misunderstandings, and irrelevant annoyances.

Love life despite any conditions in **life.**

I strongly believe that love is the ultimate purpose of life, because whenever we're truly in love with being alive, life always, yes always, loves us back. Our hearts become healed, problems are solved, questions are answered, opportunities present themselves, and possibilities appear when we appreciate, value, respect, honor, and love life. And since life is necessarily filled with people, we need to show people the same respect and try to understand them through the lens of Love.

Why I Wrote This Book

Since young people are impressionable and many just don't have the guidance they need to achieve any goals or dreams, I initially wanted to write this book geared toward helping young people because I'm committed to make a huge difference in their lives. But as I got into the writing, I realized that anyone could use these tools to improve their lives to Love Life, so I adjusted my intention and designed this book for all people of all ages that truly want to achieve self-fulfillment, peak performance, and optimal living.

If this is who you are and you are ready to transform yourself and your life, here is your blueprint.

I'm John Diggs, a former professional athlete turned businessman, and currently an entrepreneur with a mission to help you understand the innate wisdom you have within you and better understand the powers of:

- Beliefs

- Identity

- Decisions

- Desires

- Imagination

- Inspiration

- Action

- Gratitude

- Awareness

- Flexibility

- Happiness

I truly believe Love Life! Can You DIGG It? will have a great impact on the upcoming generation of minds and will be a book that you will pass over to your friends and down to your children when they are ready. Sooner rather than later.

Introducing the Can You DIGG It? System

For the last 10 years, I have been developing a philosophy, a way of being, a system of thought that has enabled me to go from being essentially homeless, virtually jobless, and even almost life-less to now experiencing excellent health, extraordinary wealth, enormous success, and extreme happiness.

DIGG It! I've made the question "Can You Digg It?" mean much more than a cool question by the cool from the 70s and a great wordplay on my last name, Diggs. Please let me explain.

The first two chapters are designed to give you an appreciation of the gifts of Love and Life, which we can all have in equal measure.

But if we don't recognize these gifts within us and coming from others, we're not ready to receive all the things that come with them. I intend to open up your mind to these gifts and show you how to be ready to receive when opportunities arise.

The first word, "Can", stands for **The Power of Belief** because what we can or cannot do, what we think is possible or impossible is directly related to our beliefs. What we believe is true, about ourselves and our immediate world, becomes true. This is the first power. Whether you can Love Life or cannot Love Life is determined by your beliefs. Your beliefs are what shape and control all your thoughts, feelings, actions, and reactions. These beliefs are a powerful force in our lives but can be detrimental without the right skills, tools, and understanding of how they came to be.

"Beliefs have the power to create and the power to destroy." (Tony Robbins)

Tony Robbins was absolutely right. Beliefs can help us create a life we love but can also destroy all the love in our lives. Beliefs are very powerful, more powerful than you might imagine. You must believe you can love life before you actually will love life.

The second word, "You", stands for the second power: **The Power of Identity**. The most important beliefs we have are beliefs about who we are. "I AM" is one of the most powerful combinations of words because what comes after those words will become who you will be.

In my second book, I AM, the companion to Love Life! Can You Digg It? I outline for you exactly what I did to go from being virtually wifeless, family less, homeless, completely broke, with no car and no job to now having the wonderful life I have today. Got my wife back, family back, a beautiful home and making a solid high six figure income for the last ten years. I haven't made any of this up just to fill a book. I actually took all the steps I'm sharing with you. It took work and it took time. And I am truly

BlessednGrateful to finally be able to share all that I've learned and I'm learning with you now.

Understand first and foremost that I am, you are, we all are spiritual beings connected to a higher power that gives us the ability to Love. This power is inherent within you, but if you're living from a place of inauthenticity, putting on a game face in your personal life, you haven't tapped into your potential; you don't yet know what you're capable of because you don't yet know who YOU are.

The truth is I am, you are, we are capable, hopeful, and worthy of loving life because we've all been born blessed with the third power: **The Power of Decision.** You must take responsibility for your own fate from this moment forward and decide what you want from life. What is it that you want? Why do you want that?

Once you decide what you want and understand why you want that, then you can focus on achieving it. But if you don't know your "why", it will be difficult to maintain that focus. Your "why" is what you will fall back on every time you begin to lose focus. This is what is going to get you through—remembering why you're doing this.

The "D" in Can You Digg It? represents our ability to decide who we want to be. We have the power to decide what we want to do. We have the power to decide what we want to have in order to love our experience of life.

It's our ability to make decisions, by virtue of our reasoning mind, that makes us human. Each power is important in its own right, but you must decide, think for yourself. What or who do you want to be? What do you want to do? What do you want to have? Figure out WHY you want these things and the rest will fall into place. I'll show you how to do that.

"We're not the product of our circumstances.
We're the product of our decisions."

- Stephen Covey

Our decisions define our destiny. To love life, we must make a clear, unequivocal decision about who we must be in order to do all we want to do and have all we want to have.

After we've decided our desires, the next step is to utilize the fourth power: **The Power of Imagination**. This is the "I" in Can You DIGG It?

The imagination is the workshop of the mind. Imagination is the creator of everything. Some of the greatest minds who ever lived agreed with this. They knew and believed in the power of the imagination.

Albert Einstein believed imagination provided a preview of life's coming attractions.

George Bernard Shaw believed that when we imagine what we desire, we will what we imagine, and we create that which we have willed.

We must dream, imagine, and visualize loving life; being, doing, and having what we decided. This is where you can imagine yourself being, doing, and having anything. And your why will be your inspiration to get you there, supported by your passion. I'll show you how to use your imagination and how to hone in on your passion, that thing that will keep you on track, keep you interested and Loving Life.

Once we've made a decision and imagined ourselves loving life, the most important thing do now is to…

GO!

The first "G" in Can You Digg It? is the fifth power: **GO! The Power of Going with Action**.

Action has the magical ability to turn dreams into reality. Picasso believed action is the foundational key to all success.

"Go confidently in the direction of your dreams."

- Henry David Thoreau

It's time to live the life you've imagined. Nothing happens without action, some action by someone or something.

Now Digg this. Love is a verb. So to love life, we must be acting, going, and moving.

But love is also a noun. So when we are going in the direction of our dreams, making decisions, and creating our lives, we are not only experiencing the action of loving life, we are giving and receiving love, the emotion.

In gratitude, be thankful and communicate with the God in you, the inner wisdom, knowing that you have all that's necessary to get you where you want to be, but you must acknowledge and validate that wisdom, that inner strength.

The second "G" in Can You DIGG It? represents **The Power of Guiding Your Gift**, the sixth power.

When moving into action, we must make sure our thoughts, our feelings, and our behaviors are guided towards what we decided to be, do, and have in order to love life. Everything must happen based in this moment, not in the past. Every thought, feeling, and action must move us toward our desires.

Awareness of your thoughts and feelings and actions will allow you to see when you're moving away from your goal. Awareness allows you to change your thoughts, feelings, and behaviors immediately. And so you must be flexible to adjust and adapt to circumstances to stay on track. I'll show you how to do this.

The main factors behind success in anything and everything are imagination, self-control and flexibility.

"The mental flexibility of the wise man permits him to keep an open mind and enables him to readjust himself whenever it becomes necessary to adapt to a change."

- Malcolm X

Life is a continuous process of adjustments to change. Thus, we must consistently guide ourselves until we experience Internal Transformation.

Once we are able to transform our inner self through the first six powers: changing your beliefs, understanding your identity, making the right decisions, using your imagination, going in the direction of your dreams, and guiding your gift along the right path, you will achieve the seventh power: **The Power of Happiness**. This is the actual experience of being, doing, and having what you decided. And this is also the It in Can You DIGG It? You will have achieved IT!

IT is achieving the goal. IT is realizing the dream. And this equates to being in love with life!

Let me give you a short Can You DIGG It? example that I hope resonates with you.

Let's say you Can believe in the importance of great health because You Are someone who would like to love life as long as possible. So you Decide to get fit and lose ten pounds. You begin to Imagine yourself ten pounds lighter, feeling fit, and looking good. Then you Go get a gym membership and start to consistently Guide yourself by making sure you go to the gym regularly. At some point you'll transform internally, your mind set will become one of Belief that has happened for you. You must and you will experience the Happiness of losing ten pounds and loving life.

Can You DIGG It? I knew that you could. I'm on a divine mission to love my life by helping you love your life. Therefore, I sincerely hope you will allow me to challenge you, to encourage you, to lead you, to mentor you, to support you by supplying the 7 Powers of Can You DIGG It? so you will fall madly in love with your life.

Can You DIGG It? I knew that you could!

Let's stay connected. Let's help each other love this amazing experience we call life together. I intend to do my part by sharing powerful books, presentations, seminars, videos and webinars with the sincere hope that you'll be moved to do your part. Watch, Like, Friend, register, Share and subscribe all this information with anyone or any age you think will benefit from it.

What You Will Learn from this Book

This book was created to help anyone achieve self-fulfillment, peak performance, and optimal living. An unconditional Love for all of Life is the goal and Can You DIGG It? is the thought process that will get you there. It's a behavioral system and a way of Being that will get you to achieving your goal.

My mission is to improve lives through inspiration, leadership, support, and love; to encourage and enable people to passionately love the experience of life in a world that also feels, shares, and receives the love.

But this system can be used by anyone of any age at any stage of life. And it will work for you, too.

You'll learn:

- How what you believe about yourself will determine what and who you are now and what or who you will become

- How your beliefs shape your thoughts, actions, feelings, and your world.

- How your identity—how you see yourself and how others see you—is a product of what you've been indoctrinated to believe about yourself and your world

- How the decisions and choices you've made up until now have provided you with what you have or don't have

- How imagination and inspiration are a key component in creating your vision for yourself

- How nothing in life happens without action

- How your thought patterns guide your actions and reactions

- How anyone can and will learn to reconnect and develop their natural ability to love life.

- And much more...

How to Use this Book

This is a self-help book, but it's not a book where you can skip around and choose the parts that look interesting to you. Each step, each Power, builds on the one before it. You can certainly read any of the Powers out of order, but implementing them will be far less effective if you don't start with understanding the powers that preceded.

If you find yourself not Loving Life, struggling every day to find happiness or success, and blaming others or your circumstances or your upbringing for not having what you want, you need to address one or more of the Can You DIGG It? powers.

I'd pretty much hit rock bottom. I had no job after building a business and succeeding at it, my wife left me and took my kids with her, I was evicted from my home because I could no longer pay for it, and as a grown man I had to move back in with my mom. Even my car was gone.

These tools and techniques work. I've used them to create a new life—the life I want. The Life I Love. I now have what I desire. I've changed my outlook, my actions, and my circumstances. And you can too. It's as simple as thinking the thoughts, saying the words, and taking the action steps outlined for you here.

This is an easy step-by-step process for achieving goals and realizing dreams. It's not a difficult process, but it is one that requires your full attention and commitment. If you backslide, simply continue along until you master each step.

If you want to experience the joy of being alive and being fully in love with life as the amazingly wonderful passage it can be for you, I'm down, set, and ready to help you release the past, not fear the future, and embrace the present moment—the only moment that exists for us.

Can You DIGG It? I knew that you could.

1.

WHAT IS LOVE?

Love can encompass a wide range of positive feelings, including warmth and respect, friendship, joy, pleasure, and affection. It's a force of nature that we cannot deny. It's not compromised by superficial benefits or negative outcomes.

"Love takes off masks that we fear we cannot live without and know we cannot live within."

- James Baldwin

Love is our most powerful emotion. It cannot be commanded or demanded. But what is love, really? How do we define it?

According to some psychologists, the primary emotions include anticipation, joy, trust, fear, surprise, sadness, disgust, and anger. They talk about collections of these basic emotions which create what they call combined emotions, and which include optimism, **love**, submission, awe, disapproval, remorse, contempt, and aggressiveness.[1]

Since the definition of any emotion cannot truly be expressed, but is in fact guessed at, then individual emotions themselves cannot truly be defined.

In its pure form, love may not be an emotion at all.

"Your task is not to seek for love, but merely to seek and find all the barriers within yourself that you have built against it." (Rumi)

The part of the brain that involves feeling is an area where neurologists and scientists have gone with some success. Brain scans show different values of heat occurring during different emotional states. Emotions are complex and are usually a subjective response, as in love or fear.

Something that is subjective is something that is "based on or influenced by personal feelings or opinions." So your emotional reaction to something is based on how you feel about a situation, not on facts. Your subjective response to something is based on your own experience with similar situations.

But DIGG this: the highest measurable frequency scientists have been able to record occurs when a person is in a state of love. This would indicate that love itself may be a basic emotion, not a combination of joy and acceptance. In fact, it may not be an emotion at all, as you'll learn.

Can We Choose to Love?

Let's use the emotion of trust as an example. Is it really an emotion or is it a conscious decision to take a stand of action?

Love may also be a conscious decision taken in the context of familial or romantic relationships. I can choose to not love or trust a person, and while I may be capable of choosing to trust them, can I choose to love them?

Is love an unconscious change in response to our subjective sensibility? If we choose to not love someone or something or the entire universe, must our psychological makeup replace love with fear, anger, or pensiveness?

The mind can never be completely stilled, so theoretically there must always be some emotional state of consciousness, whether evident or not.

Love is a Vibration

So what is Love? Love is definitely something we feel even though it may be something that most people cannot define. It can be considered the opposite of fear. But the ultimate reality is that Love is a vibration. What does that mean?

Most of us have heard or even used some form of the expression, "I'm getting good vibes from him." You might say or feel this from someone you take an instant liking to. Or "I'm getting bad vibes." This is something you might feel from a person or place that is inherently evil or extremely negative.

Every object on this planet, still or alive, has an electrical frequency. It's all around us. It's measurable in units called Hertz (Hz), and in living organisms, it's measured in Megahertz (MHz).

Your energy surrounds your physical body and can extend up to nine feet in every direction.[2,3,4] It acts as a shield from external energy. If your energy field is weak, you may have a tendency to become easily overwhelmed by outside influences. If it's overly strong, it can actually be an energy drain on others who may be weak.

Vibrations have a tendency to want to align with each other, the weaker going into sync with the stronger. When we think of this in the context of human vibrations, the weaker one will essentially be swallowed or overwhelmed by the stronger one. That's why we need to exercise humility and mercy.

At some point in this process of experiencing my 7 Powers and developing them within yourself, you'll be able to see beyond the obvious. Nothing in life will be a mystery. You'll have learned calmness in chaos, grace and delicacy in diplomacy, and relationship to all things. You'll be able to sense the vibrations of another human and implement the Four Qualities of Love I talk about further on.

"If you want to find the secrets of the Universe, think in terms of energy and frequency."

- Nikola Tesla

What did Tesla mean when he said think in terms of frequency? And what does all this have to do with Loving Life?

Let's go to a very brief study of vibrations and how the human body, which is comprised of millions of atoms, vibrates at its own unique frequency.

Cymatics, which is the study of vibration through sound, demonstrates the vibratory nature of reality—your reality; the reality of your physical body and mind. Studies of sound and vibration (frequency), when put into rhythmic patterns, have shown that our bodies instinctively understand the power of sound.

In 2010, John Hutchinson, an electromagnetic expert, successfully purified oil-infested waters in the Gulf of Mexico following the BP oil spill by using 528 Hz and other Solfeggio frequencies. The water was purified and the results were certified and confirmed by an independent lab.[5]

In the 1930s, Dr. Royal R. Rife cured 16 of 16 cancer patients by using a hand-built frequency device and using the frequencies of 432 Hz and 528 Hz. In Pythagorean math, 528 resolves to a 6, the icon for physical manifestation, and this sacred geometry is consistent with the structure of DNA. These vibrations resonate with the human body.[6,7]

This should give you a good idea of the power of vibration and frequency.

You can put this to practical use by visualizing your thoughts plans, and goals while listening to background music. This is not just some hokey new age notion. It's backed by solid science.

But be careful about the kind of music you listen to.

Original classical music symphonies were created in 432 Hz, but in Nazi Germany, Joseph Goebbels changed the original scale from 432 Hz to 440 Hz, an unnatural tone that is not found any-where in nature. They found that this stifled creativity and dulled emotions, thus they were able to keep the masses under a certain amount of control.

Later, the Rockerfeller Foundation adopted this technique and set it as the official scale for music. Of course, this information was kept from the public.[8]

In Chapter 6: The 4th Power: I: The Power of Imagination, I dis-cuss how binaural beats can help you with this. Binaural beats[9] are sound wave therapy that works with frequency patterns in the brain, and can be obtained using simple audio tracks and headphones. (You can also learn more in Appendix II: Meditation & Binaural Beats)

If certain frequencies can have a negative effect on our emo-tions, then other frequencies can have the opposite effect. The vibrations of the emotions we emit have a physical impact on the world around us. We literally attract things based on the strength of our emotions.

In a fascinating experiment which you may have seen or heard about, sand was placed on an ordinary plate. When the plate was made to vibrate using a tone generator and using varying frequencies, different geometrical patterns emerged.[10]

In his famous mind-blowing water experiment, Dr. Masaru Emoto exposed water to certain frequencies and then froze the water. He then took a high-powered camera to take pictures of the frozen water. What he found was that the water that was exposed to Mozart and Beethoven (432 Hz) formed beautiful geometric crystal patterns, and the water exposed to rock music (440 Hz) was distorted and looked polluted even though the water came from the same source.[11]

The human body is more than 70% water. Think about that. If frequencies effect water in this way, what are they doing to your body?

Why am I telling you all this?

Because understanding the dynamic nature of frequencies (vibrations) will allow you to unlock doorways within you, releasing blockages and negativity, and allowing your innate freedom of creative and spiritual expression to come forward.

Everything operates on resonance. Vibration is Life. Words have their own energy, and a negative mind can make you sick because of the energetic vibration of your words and thoughts.

We are vibrational beings. If the body remains at a vibrational dissonance, that dissonance will continue to poison and invite disease at the worst, and at best leave you with negativity and a life that is non-productive. A life that you don't love. Every day will seem like a struggle.

Modern technology, because of its ability to go worldwide and reach many millions of individuals, has the potential to be the most powerful agent on the planet to amplify love and harmony among all living things.

And it all begins with our thoughts; our awareness of them and the direction we take them.

"Loving people live in a loving world. Hostile people live in a hostile world. Same world." (Wayne Dyer)

The Four Qualities of Love

When I talk about love, I'm not necessarily referring to romantic love or familial love. I'm talking about the universal quality of Love. But regardless of how or whom you love, there are four essential qualities that comprise Love.

1. **Kindness**

   In Buddhism, the primary meaning of Love is Friendship; a love that has the intention and capacity to offer joy and kindness to others.

2. **Compassion**

   We are not required to suffer in order to relieve someone's suffering. By retaining clarity, calmness, and strength we can transform the situation and bring them joy.

3. **Joy**

   True love brings joy to the ones we love and to ourselves.

4. **Equanimity**

This requires us to develop a balanced mind. To become non-reactive. To see external reality as transient. It teaches us to put ourselves in the other person's shoes. To treat one another impartially.

When we embody these four qualities, we can experience true love.

"True love has the power to heal and transform the situation around us and bring a deep meaning to our lives."

– Thich Nhat Hanh

Here's a story[12] which was told by author Thich Nhat Hanh, a Vietnamese monk and scholar. In this situation, applied Love and Understanding to a potentially volatile event. I've condensed it quite a bit but it clearly and quite dramatically illustrates how we can attract what we intend to attract and how misplaced fear can create potentially dramatic results.

"One day during the Viet Nam War, I was sitting in a vacant air-field in the highlands of Vietnam. I was waiting for a plane to go to North Vietnam to study a flooding situation and help bring relief to the flood victims. The situation was urgent, so I had to go in a military cargo plane. An American officer was also waiting there for his plane. There were only the two of us.

"I saw that he was a young officer and I immediately had compassion for him, so out of that compassion I said, 'You must be very afraid of the Viet Cong' (the Vietnamese communist guerillas).

"What I said abruptly watered the seed of fear in him. He touched his gun and asked me, 'Are you a Viet Cong?' Before coming to Vietnam, these officers were taught that anyone could be Viet Cong, so that fear inhabited every American soldier.

"They knew that even a child or a monk could be a guerilla. They saw enemies everywhere. I knew I had to be very calm. I breathed deeply. 'No, I am waiting for my plane to go to Danang to study the flooding and see how I can help."

"My sympathy came through in my voice. As we talked, I was able to communicate that I believed the war had created a lot of victims, both Vietnamese and American. He calmed down visibly and I knew I was safe.

"I was safe because I had enough lucidity and calm to project my true intent to him. If I'd acted out of fear, he would have reacted out of fear and may have shot me."

This story demonstrates how fear, the opposite of love, can inform our reactions, and how our thoughts control everything we do.

Fear keeps us focused on the past because that was our experience. We fear what we do not know. To make the most of your passionate path, and to experience self-love and universal love, you must make changes in your perception, your outlook, and your ingrained beliefs about the world around you. (I talk about this in-depth in Chapter 3: The 1st Power: CAN: The Power of Beliefs). That's the only way to discover all the good that will come of it, and you may find yourself saying, "What took me so long?"

All you need is Love! Can You DIGG It? I knew that you could!

2.

LEARNING TO LOVE LIFE

"Be the change you wish to see in the world."

– Mahatma Gandhi

Life is precious and uncertain. If we can Love every second of it, regardless of whether we're going through good or bad times, how much better would that be?

It's no longer a secret that we're all made of energy. And although all energy is fundamentally the same, not all energy holds the same power. Life is pure energy, and pure energy is malleable to human intention and expectation.

Thought is a product of that energy, and though energy is thought to be the new mind, where does the mind begin? Where does life begin?

The mind is thought to be in our energy fields. No surprise there! It's in our DNA and our electrical brain activity.

On the basis of this vision of the human mind, that everything including you is a frequency of vibration (has 'vibes'), you can choose what to expose yourself to and you can manipulate your energy to behave the way you want it to behave.

So what does that mean? It means there is more than one way to create, and you are the creator. This is where your world becomes observer created.

Your Observer Created World

"Ours is a world where people don't know what they want but are willing to go through hell to get it."

- Don Marquis

Nothing exists outside this moment. Thought is an evolutionary process, so your personal history can be viewed as being fluid because your perception of it can be changed. What you felt about a situation when you were five years old might be viewed differently today, when you're fifteen, eighteen or twenty-two years old.

Every thought pattern you are currently subjecting yourself to is the result of the emotion you attached to an event when it occurred, and that emotion is what caused it to stay with you.

You have the power to observe your world with detachment, replace unworthy repeating thought patterns created by past experiences, and change your perception of your reality.

The shifting states of consciousness that once governed you will now be shifted by you. You can consciously take on the chosen characteristics of your awareness. By your own obser-vations and development of thought, your world will become observer created.

This might be a bit difficult to grasp right now. It simply means that because thoughts are always occurring, if you're aware of them, you can change those thoughts to "better" thoughts. You can choose what to think about and develop and guide them to benefit your goals rather than tear you down.

Gaining insight into the world around you requires you to empa-thize with that world. You cannot live in isolation. By following the principles and processes laid out for you here, you can bring sta-bility, clarity and wellbeing to your body, mind and spirit resulting in creative happiness and health.

In other words, you have the ability to work with your own internal energies (energy manipulation) to enhance that energy and your well-being. If you begin there and work through the rest of the Powers in the order they're presented, you'll succeed in having manipulated your thoughts to the point where you experience a Love for Life like never before. If you don't get it right now, you will. Keep reading.

When Science Gets in the Way

Science frames the world we live in. So what can it tell us about the nature of Life?

I've already demonstrated the benefits of science in giving us an understanding of how atoms vibrate at a frequency and comprise everything in the Universe. But science has also established some assumptions that are causing great problems for those who have not explored beyond the boundaries of scientific thinking.

Shifting these assumptions could bring humanity great resolve and provide solutions to our cultural differences, anxieties, behaviors, the way we communicate, and may even change our ideals and values. It will certainly change our perception of the universe, our world, and each other.

What are these assumptions?

1. **Our understanding of the physical universe. The assumption is that only physical matter is primary.**

   Although science has presented the world as being made entirely of energy, where hard matter does not exist and everything is just atoms vibrating at incredible speed, they've ignored the relevance and potential power of energy in guiding our lives. By leaving energy out of the equation, science has missed the most important factor in mankind's potential: spirituality. This non-tangible element is unique to humans. And it's what defines us. This brings us back to vibes. If your energy is negative, you won't have much going on in the way of spirituality. By that, I don't mean religion. I mean being in touch with the collection of thoughts and feelings that make YOU; that make your LIFE what it is.

2. **We're equivalent to genetic automatons. The assumption is that our genes control us, we don't control them, and we're therefore victims of our heredity; our destiny is fixed.**

   This is completely false. Our condition has more to do with our environment than our genetics. This has been proven in many ways, but one of the most popular examples is the 'nature-nurture' experiment done with identical triplets.

   Separated at birth and raised in three very different environments, three boys were reunited in their late teens to find they had many of the same interests, a fact that leaned toward the genetic dominance side of the debate. But because of their varied upbringing, as they aged, they became very different people. The nurture side of the equation seemed to overwhelmingly be the most powerful determinant of their destiny.

Professor Tim Spector, head of twin research at King's College London, tells us more. His studies have uncovered many examples of identical twins who have been raised together, in the same household, and whose early life experiences were very similar, but who still evolved into very different people, with very different personalities and careers.[13]

Spector believes epigenetics is the answer to how this is possible. Epigenetics is the study of how genes express themselves; it's the study of modifications of gene expression as opposed to altering the genetic code itself.

Put simply, instead of splicing genes to change behavior or outcomes, adjustments to environment can cause genes to react differently than they would have without that adjustment.

Things like diet, illnesses, drugs, smoking and other factors can produce temporary alterations in the behavior of genes and have major health and behavioral consequences.

And that's good news. It means that because energy is malleable to human thought and intention, we have the power to alter our lives. It's all about learned behaviors, which are a product of our thoughts and our beliefs.

3. **Darwinian Theory (Law of Evolution by Natural Selection).** The assumption is that life is a struggle for survival.[14]

    Each individual is trying to be the best while pushing down others to stay alive in this struggle.

Darwinian Theory states that "all species of organisms arise and develop through the natural selection of small, inherited variations that increase the individual's ability to compete, survive, and reproduce."

Because we're in a constant state of trying to survive, we must compete with others for the job, the girl, the bid, the offer, the sale... This creates constant competition. Competition is war. We even compete against nature itself as though nature is separate from us. We've tried to control nature and look what we've done with it.

Nature always strives to create balance. Each new organism throws the balance off, so nature brings into existence a new organism to return the balance. But even that new organism will throw the balance off. Each new organism is more powerful in controlling and keeping the balance. Humans are here by nature's intent to bring harmony and balance to the world, but we became so powerful that we began to override just about everything, even each other. We lost our mission of creating balance.

We've tilted it so far off that we're facing our own extinction.

How Does Perception Fit In?

Our perception of our environment (our personal world), how we see that world and what we think about it is called our world view. I believe, most importantly, that it is our world view that plays a particularly large role in how our genes express. Ninety percent or more of disease is connected to how we live in the world because how we live in the world is altering our genetic activity.

What we know and believe about ourselves and our world has formed our reality.

If what we know and believe has formed our reality, is it possible for you to accept that if you change what you believe you can change that reality to one of your choosing? Read on. Chapter 3: The 1st Power: CAN: The Power of Beliefs will blow your mind and change everything you've ever believed about yourself and your reality.

The Prison of Your Social Conditioning

In the movie, The Matrix, a portion of mankind is living a simulated reality created by conscious reasoning machines. This virtual activity can only take place by stealing the bioelectric power of humans, with its sole purpose being to subdue mankind into passivity and suppression in order to feed itself.

If this seems familiar, it's because social conditioning has made your life like that Matrix; you spend your days feeding your life force into the machine, giving it your energy. You dump it all into the machine of social conditioning. This is like the cave, the 'social condition' created in Aristotle's theory.

The mind, like the science fiction Matrix, has a tendency to use whatever it can for its own agenda, so if your emotions are fragile, for example, your mind will 'protect' itself by shutting down to anything that might hurt you emotionally. If you've been embarrassed by a failure, your mind will prevent you from engaging in anything that resembles that experience. But once again, these are all illusions.

We are constantly decorating our prisons...

...improving the masks we wear, putting up fronts, and trying to survive within the parameters set up by the social conditioning Matrix. However, regardless of how you've been conditioned to hide yourself, to fit it, true nature does not change. You are not the mask you wear. That true nature is what you must strive to rediscover by getting rid of your existing illusions.

There are endless levels of mind.

Human consciousness is a continuum, timeless, the Imminent Self, simply I Am or anata - no self. Here is where you are able to see outside your conditioning and recognize the illusions for what they are. There is a constant, intelligent inner energy in you which, when it finds the awakening from your mask, is freed from societal conditional patterns and becomes available to be directed by the soul, your true nature.

It's in this way that you can manifest the illusion that suits you best. You will have literally changed your energy; now the illusion is observer created, with you being the observer, not the victim of your social conditioning reflected as thoughts that emanate from both the unconscious and subconscious portion of your mind, thoughts which are replayed over and over again because this is what was familiar, even though it may have been counterproductive.

And just like in The Matrix, once you're aware of how the machine works, you will be able to shape it to your desire; you'll be reawakened with the capacity to perceive and command the matrix, and you will be shown a universe in which anything is possible.

Can You DIGG It? I knew that you could!

3.

THE FIRST POWER: CAN: THE POWER OF BELIEFS

"A man is but a product of his thoughts. What he thinks, he becomes."

- Mohandas K. Gandhi

Plato had a theory that people live their lives as though they're inside a cave, watching the shadows in front of them made by whatever was passing by the fire behind them. They were born in the cave, yet they instinctually knew there was more outside the cave. This was demonstrated by whatever was passing by the fire, those things that were not inside the cave with them but seemingly existed with a life that came from another source. But they were immobilized by their fear of what those things might be, so they refused to 'think outside the box'. In fact, they were incapable of it because the cave was all they knew.

Those are your paralyzing thoughts.

You may have feelings of déjà vu or yearnings that you 'can't quite put your finger on'. You have a longing to do something, whatever that is for you, yet you can't seem to find your way out of the cave. You know there's more out there but you cannot or refuse to let go of what's familiar, whether it's comforting or not.

You can think of the cave as your primal instincts; survival is the first thing you would consider, but there would be no actual 'considering'. It's just how nature works. First we survive, then we strive for something more. Or at least that should be the plan. But there are endless levels of mind that can take you places you could not possibly dream of if you stay within the confines of the cave of shadows. And those can be shadows of your past experiences, traumas, lost or forgotten dreams, fears, or even something in your DNA memory handed down to you by a potentially unlimited line of ancestral energy.

The world of thinking is the only world humans know...

...yet they are afraid of the dark, of the unknown, of other people, of leaving what's familiar, and of exploring any possibility of what's achievable. The real tragedy, however, is that people are afraid of the light. The light shines on flaws and exposes your weaknesses, but it also illuminates the illusions that you may have been living with; the demons. There are no demons except for the ones you've created in your mind.

You are not "in" a prison; you are the prison, and that prison is your own consciousness; your thoughts, fears, memories, and emotions, all emanating from your subconscious mind.

So how do you break free from the prison that is you?

Begin by understanding that in order to ascertain the truth, you must doubt everything because everything in the mind is an illusion. If you try to fight against the prison, the illusion becomes real, a living nightmare, and you'll be running from the shadows forever.

Understand that by freeing your mind from all those limiting illusions manifested as thoughts, you can create any 'illusion' you want.

How You Think is as Important as What You Think

"For as a man thinketh in his heart, so is he."
(Proverbs 23:7)

"Be transformed by the renewing of your mind."
(Romans 12:2)

"What the mind of man can conceive and believe, it can achieve."

- Napoleon Hill

These Natural Laws are as ancient as man and have been paraphrased by many. They exemplify the concept of how thoughts and emotions make us what we are. What you think about and what you conceive in your mind reflects in your actions and behavior. How you behave is an extension of your Pure Heart, the seat of emotion. I'm not talking about the physical heart, the one that resides in your chest. I'm referring to the Spirit.

But how did you begin to think the way you do? When did your world change? What influenced the way you think today? How did your emotions, heart and Spirit become what they are? Surely you were not born to mistrust and hate others or devalue yourself.

As babies, our world—the environment we live in and experience—is decided by our parents. As small children, we're still relatively fearless in that we have no awareness of injustice, injury, politics, invasion, privacy, or context, among other things. Our only context is the world in which we currently live, the world our parents created. This may be a happy place or a negative place, a world primarily of abuse, discipline, creativity, chaos, affluence, culture, poverty, art, music, dancing, nature, sports, or any number of other circumstances. It doesn't matter. This is all we know. This is our world view. These are the imprints that are beginning to take hold in our mind.

Dr. Bruce Lipton, author of Biology of Belief and the Honeymoon Effect, says, "The first six years of a child's life, the conscious part of the brain is not primarily functioning. A child is observing the environment just like a television camera, recording everything. The child observes and gauges the world through the parents' responses, and uses them as a reference point."[15]

As we grow and have more social contact with other children, we gain more imprints. If our early life was positive, constructive, and supportive, we're able to interact in a confident way. If, up to that point, we had to constantly defend our toys from being broken by other siblings or the neighbor kids, another learned behavior, than we may find ourselves being possessive of our toys in preschool. We won't want to share because our experience has been that sharing causes damage to our stuff, and this imprint will follow us into adulthood.

A kind and patient teacher will show us that this isn't always true, but these teachers are not common, so most of us go on to gain new imprints while the old ones take root. The same holds true for everything we do, whether it's in relationships, job success, family life, possessions, money, respect, love, creativity, or anything else you can think of.

What you know is going to be what you expect and very likely what you'll get.

The way you've experienced life in the past is the way you believe life is and will continue to be. The "better lives" of celebrities, musicians, sports figures, and others is a fantasy for you. You can dream about it forever, but it won't materialize for you because you don't know how to use the tools and knowledge within you, the tools and knowledge we all have, the gifts from the Universe.

But you will know how to use that knowledge. You'll develop and nurture that knowledge by following the 7 Powers outlined in this book.

I'm not talking about governments, institutions, and organizations which have largely been created by the few to allegedly benefit the many. I'm talking about the system of Universal Organization, the Laws which govern all living things.

The good news is that what you now know—or what you think you know—can change in an instant. Knowledge is as fluid as the context within which it's viewed.

At one time the world was flat. You know now that it was never really flat, that's just what people believed back in the days before someone showed them differently. Nothing has physically changed, only the context and perspective with which the planet is viewed.

Quantum theory is little understood by many, even among those within this field of research. It's a theory about the magnitude of energy as it relates to the frequency of the radiation it represents. This theory of matter and energy is beyond the understanding of most people, but it's not beyond our imagination to believe that someday we'll all be living from that point of view. It'll be as common as knowing our planet is round.

If you understand how assumption and perspective can change thinking, you'll begin to see that what you think–the thoughts you have–are created by you. They may be influenced by the world around you and reflect what you see and hear, but your imagination and awareness of consciousness–how you change your thoughts and bend them to your will–will determine your ultimate perspective.

You can think anything and assign any meaning to your thoughts and experiences, and in this way, your world becomes a conscious manifestation of your own making rather than a world created by a lack of input or information.

Catastrophic Thinking & Learned Helplessness

Stress has always been around. It's a normal psychological and physiological reaction to the demands of life. People experience severe stress-inducing challenges every year and many have some type of stress every day.

In looking at the causes of stress, remember that your brain comes hard-wired with an alarm system for your protection. When it perceives a threat, it signals your body to release a burst of hormones to fuel your capacity for a response.

This has been labeled the "fight-or-flight" response. Once the threat is gone, your body is meant to return to a normal relaxed state. Unfortunately, the nonstop stress of modern life means that your alarm system rarely shuts off.

Most of us have lived with minor stresses for so long we simply don't recognize the changes in our bodies as being a result of that stress. And it can affect your thoughts, feelings, and behavior.

The body responds to physical and mental stressors in much the same way it does to injuries, electric shock, and harmful environmental toxic substances. If left unchecked, it can contribute to high blood pressure, heart disease, obesity, and diabetes, and it will have a major effect on longevity.

So what is fight of flight?

The fight or flight response at the core of our brain is a survival mechanism, something left over from the days when man had to deal with stressful situations like fighting wild animals with handmade weapons. He could either fight the animal or run from it. He didn't have to think about natural health, it just came... well, naturally.

During times of increased stress, the liver and pancreas will dump enormous amounts of sugar and insulin into the bloodstream as a response to the emergency. This served the caveman well. He was pumped up to either fight or run, and whatever he chose to do, he used this excess sugar.

When we face an emergency or dangerous situation, muscle tension, breathing, and heart rate increase, blood races to the heart and brain from other organs, oxygen increases in the brain, and blood sugar level rises. Adrenaline, cortisol, and other hormones are released.

Today, we have no outlet for these excesses so they turn to anger, frustration, and both physical and emotional stress.

Made-to-order stress

And it's just as often not the threat itself that causes stress but the perception of the stressor or threat.

For instance, a dog can approach two different people and one may act in fear, prompting the fight or flight mechanism while the other may feel glad thinking about petting the animal and causing "feel good" hormones to increase.

This essentially suggests that most modern stress is often self-induced.

Remember that first time you got pulled over by the police? Or that big boss who came into the room yelling at everyone? What about when your seventeen-year-old son got his driver's license and took the car out for the first time? Tell me that didn't create just a little bit of stress for you. These situations are more than just perceived threats. Unless you were actually the police officer, the big boss, or the seventeen year old kid.

Worry is a stress that is sometimes legitimate. When our teenage driver is out for the first time on his own, there is normally a certain amount of parental concern.

But when it comes to stress, your body cannot tell the difference between what is actually happening and what we think may happen. So even when the threat is not real, emotional stress occurs and affects the body.

The process of worry is the same whether large or small. We project what may happen in the future and assess whether or not we have the resources needed to cope with anticipated outcomes.

Properly placed, this is useful because we can forecast with some accuracy what we may soon need. We do this through our experience and intellect. You know that you need to study for a test. You may be worried about getting a passing grade, but you eliminate some of that worry by being prepared; by studying.

With a few bad experiences in our history, however, we may get into the habit of always predicting bad outcomes. This is called catastrophic thinking.

Learned helplessness is a passive reaction to situations we can't control or think we can't control.

Both catastrophic thinking and learned helplessness are stresses to which your body responds with inflammation. You can learn to train your brain so that your natural reactions are a healthy response instead of one which causes chronic conditions.

What to Do

- Recognize you may have a problem with stress or worry. It would be foolish to ignore real danger signals, but most of the things we worry about never happen. Train yourself to appraise situations correctly.

- Exercise is the best way to discharge excess hormones. Even three deep breaths from the diaphragm can reduce the anxiety you feel under stress. Take some time before making decisions.

- Appreciate all the happy moments you have enjoyed in your life and everything you have been grateful for receiving.

- Set aside time for loved ones, meditation, naps, or just watching the stars.

- Anticipate some setbacks. Be realistic about the time it takes to complete tasks and schedule in some slack time.

- Don't aim for perfection.

- Provide extra time when driving to work or school in the morning. Leave early and make it a habit to do everything calmly. Don't get caught up in road rage.

- Simplify and de-clutter your life. Throw out or give away old items which are no longer used.

- Learn to respond to your phone when it's convenient for you. Just because someone has texted you does not mean you have to answer immediately.

- Limit your time on social media.

- Learn to say "No" if it's going to mean taking on too many responsibilities.

- Take time to play. Laughter and a sense of humor are powerful tools to make life's challenges more manageable.

- Don't overreact. Take a deep breath and act in self-control.

- Look at solutions instead of problems.

- Learn to speak softly. As you quiet down your voice you actually relax the rest of your body and your mind as well.

- Don't spend time with people who are negative. Optimism can help you live about seven years longer.

Many situations cannot be changed by your actions so simply changing your perception or attitude toward them will help.

Remember the Serenity Prayer:

"Grant me the courage to change the things I can, the serenity to accept the things I cannot, and the wisdom to know the difference."

- Reinhold Niebuhr

Shifting From Instability & Chaos to Flow

Focused human intention is the cornerstone of genetic self-healing and manifestation for just about any way you want your life to go. The wisdom of healing— cellular wisdom—is undeniable. And in the same way our DNA has been left out of our current focus, we can use focus and mindfulness to bring it back to the center of our lives, where it can continue to edify every physical aspect of our being.

So if the human body can innately heal itself, why then should we not be able to bring a shift in our mental healing? When I talk about mental healing, I mean healing or shifting the way you think. Remember, every thought you make becomes part of you, of who you are and who you will become because of the energetic vibrations those thoughts contain.

Many of us are no longer capable of internally stimulating these changes without some type of retraining. We're out of touch with our own ability to do this. But there are means of developing your intuitive senses that will work to bring you back into the light, the light of creation, where you will relearn the fine art of living in the true sense of the word.

Believing is the first step to change, for what is in the mind's eye, what is conceivable, is already possible or already exists. The truth of your existence lies deep within you, waiting for you to discover it.

Astonishingly, studies[16] on comatose patients who showed no brain activity and who were given medication to bring them deeper into the coma, showed peculiar and unexplainable waveform activity in the hippocampus, the region of the brain responsible for emotion and long-term memory. Remember, vibrations appear as waves. Researchers believe that one possible reason for this is that silencing the brain in all other areas releases control over neurons in the hippocampus.

This gives us a hint of the far reaching possibilities and power within the brain, most of which is as yet unexplored. It may confirm that even after death, the energy within us continues to move and live.

Vibrating energy is always magnetizing to you, and since magnetic energy is a two-way street, you are always sending out your vibration as well. Now you will learn to direct those vibrations, and you will learn to harness incoming energy and either use it for good or deflect it away from you. And you will learn how to change the past by retraining your cellular memory and energetic frequency.

Try to think in terms of practical application. If we plug a lamp into an electrical outlet, we get light because the current is connected. The components are "talking to each other" through electrical signals.

Our cells contain measurable energy, and our thoughts, which are a product of our brain, can become "plugged in" to those cells by intentionally sending specific healing messages to them. We should expect a connection with bio-energetic results, just like an electrical current, because the mind acts as a frequency modulator in the same way that the light stored in DNA does. The information sent along the frequency holds the intention and, whether lab controlled or provided by our own internal sources, manifests as shifts in electrical properties. This is how energy brings about actual physiological changes.

- DNA stores light and emits measurable energy
- Cells auto-repair at a particular wavelength
- The body purposefully directs chemical reactions by means of electromagnetic vibrations
- Light emissions from the body follow measurable, biorhythmic set patterns by day, night, week, and month.
- Electromagnetic vibrations (biophotons) are transferred from the food we eat into our own cells.

The study of human biology must include matter and energy. The human cell is an electro-magnetic field, a fact that's supported by modern physics. This means you have the ability to create new energy all the time thereby shifting your reality.

In the same way shifts in electrical properties are found in the body, shifts in the cosmos can be made using the same electrical intention. You can shift your mindset, worldview, cells, your energy field, and ultimately the cosmos that surrounds you by tapping into the limitless power of your mind.

Through recognizing thought patterns, you can change your perception of your reality. And in changing your perception, you change the actual reality, creating a cosmic shift that now favors your experience and your intention. In this way, your thought will go from random repeating chaos to intentional flow.

Can You DIGG It? I knew that you could!

4.

THE SECOND POWER: YOU: THE POWER OF IDENTITY

"Unless you know who you are, you will always be vulnerable to what people say."

- Dr. Phil McGraw

Most of us make our decisions based on the time of day, the minutes on a clock; we live our lives dependent on the balance in our checking account, and we allow ourselves to be ruled by the decisions, traditions, and conventional modalities created by others even when, to us, they don't make sense. In those moments, we've lost touch with our own intuition. If we feel it beckoning us to another direction, we don't heed its call. We've learned to live comfortably numb in the "safe zone" where even though we may not be completely happy or fulfilled, we need to feel certain of what the days will bring. We've let others do our thinking for us. As Socrates wrote "Think for yourself."

Tony Robbins is one of the most successful motivational influencers today. Here's what he has to say about how our identity is a product of our beliefs:

"We all have an IDENTITY—a set of BELIEFS that DEFINE who we are, what we can and cannot or WILL not do. And it's based mostly on our past—some of which is painful, and some pleasurable.[17]

"Why is IDENTITY so important to dig under? Because BELIEFS about ourselves are among the strongest forces shaping our lives. BELIEFS control BEHAVIOR."

He uses the metaphor of your beliefs being a thermostat that you've set at a certain temperature, say 72 degrees. If you start to do better in life, become more successful, earn more money, and so on, your metaphorical thermostat can go from 72 to 80 to 85 and up. But your beliefs will kick in and tell you that you need to go back to 72 degrees because that's your comfort zone; that's where you 'belong'.

"When you've achieved BEYOND what you've ever dreamed of, you'll... self-sabotage."[18]

That's why it's so important to understand what you believe about yourself first. You can't change your past, but you can view it in a different light, in a way that is not limiting. You need to believe that something is possible for you, something you may not have believed before you understood how your past has limited your thinking.

It doesn't matter what you believe, but all your actions will be based on and be consistent with those beliefs. When you take responsibility for deciding what you truly want, you can begin to live authentically in your true identity.

It's Time for a Change of Perspective

Believe it or not, even with all the information and technology available to us and the exposure to the world that comes along with it, our initial and formative upbringing will still play a key role in the way we view the world.

Once the realization hits you that you are the way you are because of the culture to which you've been exposed, you can begin to learn to love yourself in much the same way you'd love any child. It's not the child's fault he or she was stifled by an overly protective and fearful parent. It's not the child's fault he learned prejudice because he was never exposed to anyone outside the class to which he was born.

It wasn't your fault as a child because you had neither the experiential knowledge nor the size and strength, in most cases, to defend yourself or think for yourself. You had instincts as a baby, but you were quickly (and most likely unintentionally) reprogrammed by your parents. Rules were set. Routines were created. The outside world crept into your child mind and began to form your identity because you were not strong enough to keep the one you already had or create your own.

A child who shows an inclination for individual thinking is labeled "willful". A student who looks out the window when he should be paying attention in class is labeled a daydreamer or as having an attention deficit. The fact is, most kids are still using their imaginations. They're not accustomed to sitting all day and trying to pay attention to subjects that are nothing more than foreign concepts. There's no practical application for them, though they're not aware this is the issue. When I was growing up, we called it boredom.

A "willful" child will continue to rebel, trying desperately to be heard, without the power to do so. Once children are sufficiently bored or have had their spirits crushed into submission, they begin to "behave" like the products of their society, robots who politely follow the status quo. If they don't, we pump them with drugs.

We all know there needs to be some order in civilized society otherwise anarchy would rule. In the wildest scenario, I believe communities would be able to deal with their most atrocious offenders in a way that would uplift the spirit rather than imprison and further diminish an already hurting soul. This concept is higher on the evolutionary thinking scale and we'll get to that later.

The bottom line is this: the condition your life is in now is your fault because you've allowed the abuse and misdirection to continue by your lack of intention. That doesn't make you a bad person, just misguided. You're still living like the helpless child, too small and powerless to be heard, and this has become your identity, to yourself and to others.

There are more than 7 billion people in the world, and everyone on Earth has a different perception of reality. Even twins have different perspectives.

What we perceive to be reality is simply a product of everything we've experienced. People suffer and fail because they refuse to budge from their staunch commitment to their beliefs, however misguided those beliefs might be. The need to be right makes everyone else wrong. And since it's very unlikely that everyone else is wrong, it creates chaos in the mind.

That was me for many years. I was often angry, frustrated, and irritated because I firmly believed my perception of reality was right everyone else was either crazy or stupid for not seeing and agreeing with my perception of reality!

And because of that, it was impossible for me to see the beauty around me and to Love Life. With a closed mind, I would never succeed at anything.

Fortunately, Grace bestowed its hand on me, and in 2003, Dr. Ron Homan changed my life forever. He opened my perception of reality by giving me a new appreciation and respect for the perceptions of reality that others might have, based on their own experiences. I talk more about how I met Dr. Holman and my incredible experience with him in my book, I AM.

It suddenly became easy for me to say, hey, you know what? You could be right. Because it's possible you heard something different than I did. Because it's possible you saw something different than I did. It is possible you thought something different than I did. It is possible you feel something different than I do.

This shift in my perception greatly minimized arguments, confrontations, upsets, and many other negative emotions and experiences I was used to having.

And it's because I realized and remembered that there are over 7.6 Billion different perceptions of reality, and mine is just one.

So how do you change your perspective when everything that has happened, all of your experiences, are part of you and always will be?

The Concept of Relativity

The way we view the world is based on a compilation of everything that we've ever experienced from birth, probably even before conception. Our thinking is shaped by the powerful conditioning we've undergone. The classic American world view, for example, tells us that if we work hard and apply ourselves, we'll get ahead. But your experience has shown you that this is only true for some. And on top of that, you don't want to work for fifty years only to receive a three percent increase in your wages each year, while time and the dreams you have for yourself and your family are passing you by.

You want some of what the "lucky few" are privileged to have. Once you learn to distinguish your world view—the context from which you live and make your decisions—you'll have given yourself the power to not only think for yourself but to move your life in the direction of that thinking. I'll get into that more in depth in Chapter 8: The 6th Power: G: The Power of Guidance and Gifts. Just remember that the laws of the system will work for you the same way they work for those who appear to be the lucky few.

In fact, they're already working in your life, but you haven't yet recognized that by not focusing your energy and consciousness on what you want to become, you became the manifestation of all the energy that you've experienced, which has developed into your current perspective, and which has formed your identity. You have subconsciously put out to the Universe everything you believe about the way things are, and this is what you get back.

I'm asking you to change the thoughts you put out so it will change what you get back.

Can You DIGG It? I knew that you could!

Take a look at the concept of relativity. This is the context in which you view and experience everything. In other words, everything in the world is relative to your own ability and circumstance. But remember, your perspective is subjective; you can change that.

You have $100 in your checking account and you feel as though you're broke because you're accustomed to having much more. Your neighbor has $100 in his checking account and is joyful because it's more than he's ever had. It's still $100 but its value is viewed differently because of its relation to what is usually known or present.

You can think of it another way. $100 won't go very far when buying a new car but it will be more than enough to buy yourself a movie ticket. The point is that the amount is irrelevant. How you view the amount is what's important.

The events of the two men, each with $100, could have another scenario. You're used to having much more but you're grateful that you still have $100 left in your checking account. Your neighbor, who now has more than he's ever had, might feel as though it's just a fluke and he'll never see that much money again. He's now depressed and angry because he's had a taste of "the good life" and fears it will soon be taken away from him.

Are you beginning to see how perspective is everything?

Using relativity, and understanding the fact that context is fluid, will help you to realize that the way things are at the present moment is not the way things must remain. Each and every moment instantly becomes part of the past.

The possibilities for creation are endless and available to us when we stop living from the context of our upbringing, our parents' views, our ancestors, our social groups, and our sense of victimization.

If you take a look at your most memorable events, whether positive or negative, you'll discover the source of both your power and your fear locked in your perception of those moments.

Looking with new eyes at the experiences that shaped you will shine a brilliant light on the person you are today, and making course corrections using this new filter will create a new reality, thereby shaping what you will ultimately become.

Perception is bound within the time frame of its occurrence.

Thought is an evolutionary process, so your personal history can be viewed as being fluid because your perception of it can be changed.

Every thought pattern you are currently subjecting yourself to is the result of the emotion you attached to an event when it occurred, and that emotion is what caused it to stay with you.

"The logic of the emotional mind is associative; it takes elements that symbolize a reality or trigger a memory of it to be the same as that reality. If the emotional mind follows this logic, things need not necessarily be defined by their objective identity; what matters is how they are perceived." (Daniel Goleman, Emotional Intelligence)

Once you're aware of your thoughts, you can essentially sit back and see where you're going and where you've been. You can observe your world with detachment, replace unworthy repeating thought patterns created by past experiences and change your perception of your reality.

Right now, you're saying, "But things happened to me in the past. Don't they count?" The answer to that question can be either yes or no. It all depends on whether or not you want them to count. It all depends on the meaning you give to anything.

The only meaning anything has is the meaning you give it.

Things happen. You don't need to understand the meaning of life to enjoy it. Sometimes it's a good idea to just let everything go, even if it's just for a day.

Who Are We, Really?

"Knowing yourself is the beginning of all wisdom."

- Aristotle

We all have three faces. A public face, used for strangers in polite society, a private face used around friends, family, and loved ones, and a personal face known only to ourselves, the face we use when no one else is around, the inner you, the person who knows all the deep secrets of your soul, the things you don't want to let out and cover up around others, even those close to you.

If you're an athlete, you may never admit you're just a little bit afraid of that 300 pound offensive tackle standing in front you on the field. That would make you appear weak. If you're a young man, you may never admit you're a little bit anxious about asking that beautiful girl out. That would make you appear to be a loser. As a student, you may never want to admit that you feel like the dumbest kid in the class, because that would make you appear like you weren't cool. If you're an employee in any field, you might not want to admit you made a mistake of any kind, because you feel it might jeopardize your position and make you less valuable to the company.

But all of those notions are in your head, in your thoughts, because somewhere down the line of your experiences, someone made you believe those things were true.

There were many times I didn't feel cool. But I put on the game face and just kept on keepin' on.

But the more we put on a face that is not authentic, the longer it will take to find that authentic you and begin to mold your life to the one you really want.

We all know people. When we meet with our friends, associates, and coworkers or when we witness a stranger's behavior in a public place, we don't usually look deep into their psyche in an attempt to understand why they are the way they are. We usually either accept or reject them, passing instant judgment based upon the particular behavior they displayed when we first met them. Sometimes we use our instincts and get an immediate good or bad vibe. A person's "vibe" is the frequency within which they're operating and the energy or qi that emanates from them, something that is measurable using scientific devices.

We all use catch words to summarily describe others - John is a hoot. Mary loves everybody. Sally is a hard nut to crack. Joe is a strict task master. Within each and every person, however, there is a personal history, a world of events of which they are the result, with DNA that has been handed down for thousands of years.

Finding Your Authentic Self

There is only one you. Stop devaluing yourself by trying to be a copy of someone else."

- Susie Clevenger

We think we know ourselves. People close to us think they know us and we think we know them. But what do you really know about yourself? I'm going to ask you to dig deeper to find out which events and people in your past contributed to who you are today.

You could call this a little bit of homework. (You can also join one of my Free Mind Mapping Webinar Sessions at johndiggs.com where I will work with you personally).

The Potential of Mind Mapping

"A Mind Map is a revolutionary thinking tool that, when mastered, will transform your life."

- Tony Buzan

The most effective way to do this homework is to create a Mind Map. Mind Maps are designed to help you process information, come up with new ideas, strengthen your memory, get the most out of your leisure time and improve the way you work.

Tony Buzan introduced Mind Maps to the world in the 1960's. In his book, Mind Map Mastery,[19] he states that "I devised the mind map initially as an innovative form of note-taking that can be used in any situation where linear notes would normally be taken, such as attending lectures, listening to phone calls, during business meetings, carrying out research and studying. However, it quickly became clear that Mind Maps can also be used for ground-breaking design and planning; for providing an incisive overview of a subject, for inspiring new projects, for uncovering solutions and breaking free from unproductive ways of thinking among many other things" He goes on to say, that Mind Maps can even be used as an exercise in their own right to give your brain a workout and boost your powers of creative thinking.

I've been Mind Mapping for over 10 years, and I'm convinced that Mind Maps are powerful tools for focusing and processing information, formulating a plan of action and getting started on new projects. In fact, Mind Mapping is a huge guiding hand in every aspect of life – and I can't recommend it highly enough.

Your Brain is a sleeping giant, and Mind Mapping is the perfect tool to help wake it up!

Here are some of the many advantages of Mind Mapping:

- Thinking: Ignite your brain, come up with fresh ideas and associations that can spark further creativity, and establish a colorful record of your thinking process.

- Learning: Works as a great study aid, useful for note-taking during classes, meetings, lectures, and for exam revision.

- Concentration: Aids in focusing closely on the task at hand, and in engaging the brain in a way that will inevitably lead to better results.

- Organizing: Great tool for organizing parties, weddings, trips, family gatherings, and even your future life.

- Planning: A tool for prioritizing your time and commitments, planning your daily, weekly, and monthly diary, and scheduling your appointments and tasks. Communication: Keeps you on track; allows you to highlight key ideas so you can get your point across effectively and precisely.

- Speaking: Keeps information at a glance; keeps presentations and speeches clear, relaxed, and dynamic.

- Leading: An excellent business tool that gives you a control desk for making sense of your internal and external universes.

- Training: Plan training programs in a quick, accessible, and customizable format.

- Negotiation: See all your options, available strategies, and potential outcomes laid out clearly on one page.

DIGG It! Mind Mapping has truly changed my life. It has enabled me to sort out my ideas and thoughts and create powerful strategies to achieve my goals and realize my dreams to Love Life.

If you only get one thing out of this book, my hope is the power of what Mind Mapping can do to improve your life. Which is why I am committed to doing all I can to introduce and coach people to become Mind Mapping Masters. Please join me for one of my free Mind Mapping Introduction webinars. Register at johndiggs. com/mindmaps

Begin by making three Maps. Take some time with these, possibly even over the course of several days or more.

You can either manually create a map on a horizontal sheet of paper, or go to MindMeister.com and sign up for a free Mind Mapping template.

I'm a partner with Mind Meister. I decided to become a U.S. partner with the Munich, Vienna based Mind Meister because, after thorough research, I've found it to be simply the best online Mind Mapping software available today.

My goal is to become a Mind Meister Top U.S. Partner, and your help in signing up for this free version is greatly appreciated. If you choose to upgrade to a paid version of Mind Meister, please enter this code (DIGGIT) for instant savings and to reward me with a referral fee. Thank you very much!

DIGG This Mind Map First

For the first Map, write "Me" or put a picture of yourself in the middle and start to think about everything you know about yourself. Create as many topics around your central image as you like, such as habits, desires, job, routines, types of people in your circle, dreams or aspirations, goals, fantasies, dislikes, talents, schooling, honors and awards, sports, your physical characteristics, your personality, and so on. Come up with as many topics as you can think of.

The more specific you can make the topics, the deeper your understanding of yourself will be. For example, one of your topics is people. Map people by name and describe them. You might state why you like them, how they make you feel, what they do for a living, and particularly your specific relationship with them.

If you've added family to your Map, state who they are, their place in the family hierarchy, how you feel about them and your impression of how they feel about you, their qualities and flaws and so on. If you've been told stories or seen pictures about distant ancestors, did that make any impression on you? Did it change your image of yourself either in how you feel about any family resemblance or due to the reputations of these people publicly or within the family tree?

Here are some examples of the exercise.

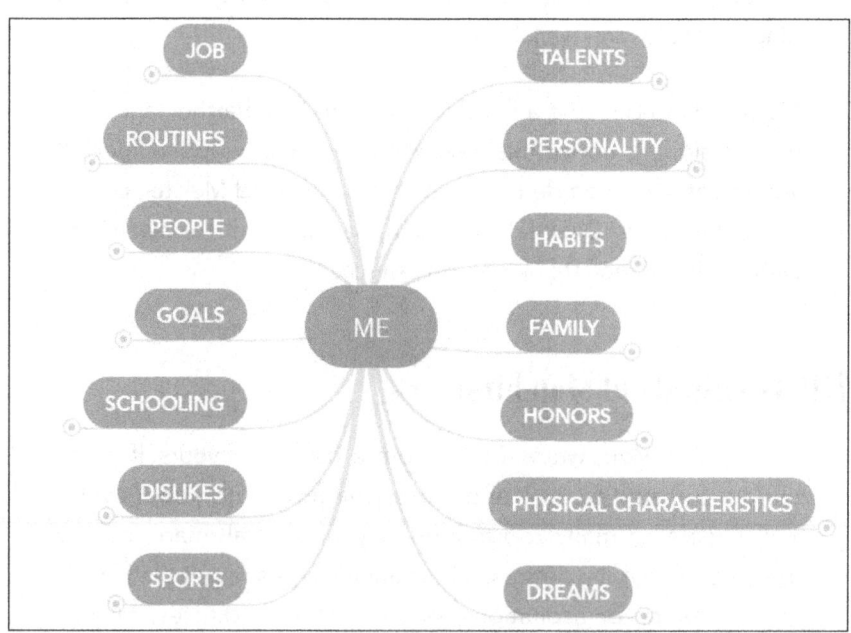

Initial Thoughts – Quickly Added Thoughts

Deeper Thoughts -- Greater Mind Map Development

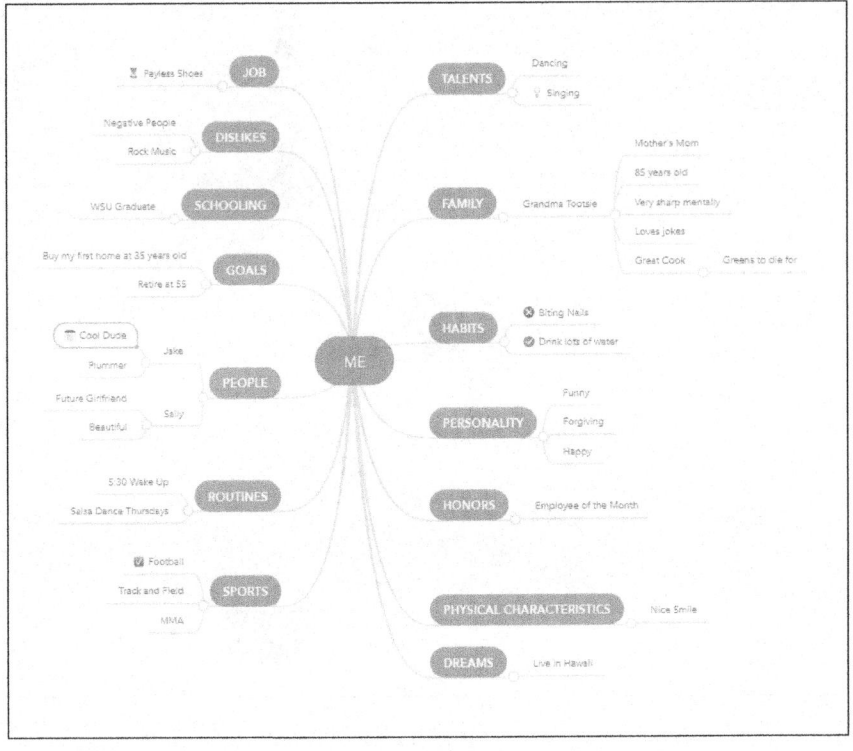

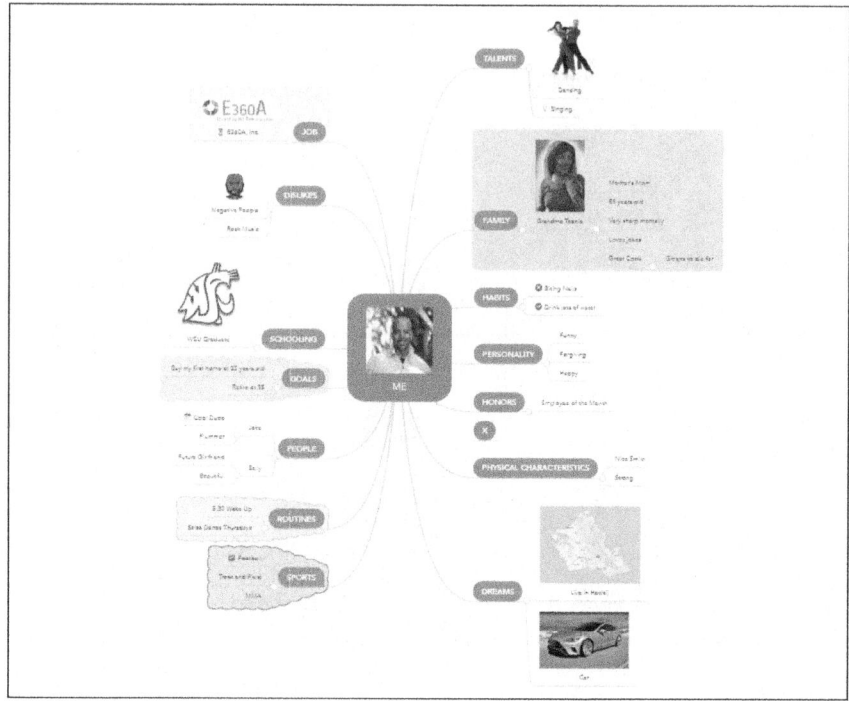

As of the writing of this book, I'm sure I have developed this Mind Map even more. Do you want to see it? And use it as a template for your own map? Great! All you need to do is email me at john@johndiggs.com with "Me Mind Map" in the subject line and I will send you a copy of this map right away. You can also find more Maps to review and/or copy at johndiggs.com/mindmaps

Your next two Maps will contain the 10 (or more) most negative and the 10 most positive people, experiences, events, or moments you can remember. These will be something or someone who was impactful to you in some way. Go back as far as you can remember and create details of the experience. Look at the people who were part of that experience and the role they played.

When you have Maps 2 and 3 completed, number them by importance in the far right column: "How strong was the impact this person or event had on me?"

*Please feel free to add colors, images and symbols to your mind maps because making your Maps more visually engaging and more interesting to your brain helps with memory and retention.

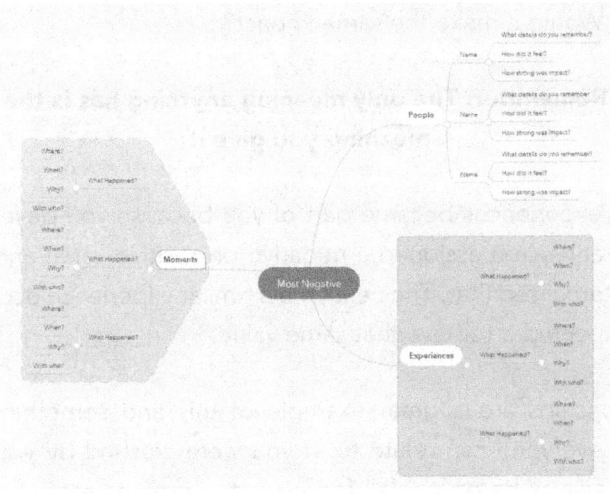

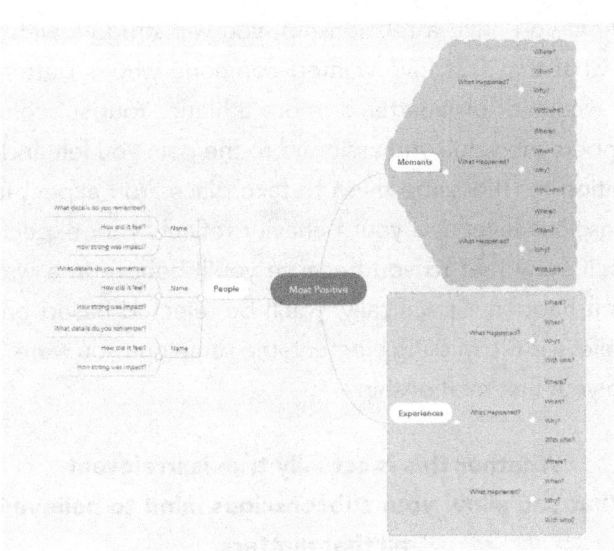

Take a good look at these Map and you'll begin to see yourself differently. Which person or event do you feel is the most important on your map?

Try to remember the emotion you attached to that event and all the others. There was emotion or it would not have impacted you one way or another. Was it positive or negative? If the exact same circumstances happened to you today, would you react differently? Would it make the same impact?

Remember: The only meaning anything has is the meaning you give it.

These experiences became part of you because you gave them importance. You assigned a negative or positive value and then you internalized that. The next time a similar experience occurred, you expected it to have that same value.

Relationships are a great example of this and something just about everyone can relate to. If you were crushed by your first love because he or she fell for a smarter, prettier, more rugged, wealthier, better educated, more athletic, or whatever person, each time you have a relationship, you will struggle with trying to be what that first love wanted–someone who is better looking or wealthier or smarter or more athletic. Your subconscious remembers the value you assigned to the pain you felt and it will be waiting for the same thing to take place. You expect it on a subconscious level and your behavior reflects your expectation. So you'll draw that to you because you'll behave in a way that makes it happen. Specifically, you'll be rejected based on what you believe is the missing element–the same one you were "missing" in your first relationship.

Whether this is actually true is irrelevant.
What you allow your subconscious mind to believe is
all that matters.

The subconscious mind does not know the difference between what's real and what's virtual. It doesn't know whether you have actually experienced something or whether you just thought about it vividly and in detail. So every time you replay an event in your mind, it reinforces it as a deeper reality.

The Law of Substitution states that if you believe something strongly enough (attach passion or emotion to it) and replay it in your mind as a recurring thought, your subconscious will believe it actually happened. It can replace an old imprint and make it weaker through lack of attention.

Michael Phelps has won fifteen Olympic gold medals and is the most decorated athlete in Olympic history. In a Forbes interview with Bob Bowman, Phelps's Olympic swimming coach, Bowman had this to say:

"For months before a race, Michael gets into a relaxed state. He mentally rehearses for two hours a day in the pool. He sees himself winning. He smells the air, tastes the water, hears the sounds, and sees the clock."

This is the Power of Imagination and the subconscious mind. Your thoughts, what you tell yourself is true, has the potential to become your reality. In Chapter 6: The 4th Power: I: The Power of Imagination, I talk more about visualizing your life, how to get into the flow zone, and how to access your point of power. I've also included a sample guided imagery (visualization) in Appendix III for you to use and practice how to do this.

The subconscious mind doesn't know the difference between what really happened and what you tell it has happened.

In a ground-breaking study,[20] researchers at the International Space Station (NASA) used computerized virtual reality scenarios designed to gather information about how perception affects us.

"Using advanced virtual reality devices, subjects were "transformed" into an animation of Sigmund Freud's body and were asked to give themselves psychological advice.

"When they listened to Freud's recorded response—which, of course, was their own response with a slightly modified voice, they had a more positive response to their own advice then when they were "themselves".

"The study, published in Nature Scientific Reports, found that the feeling of embodying someone we see as authoritative affects the way we feel and think about ourselves."

Researchers specifically chose Freud for their study because of his fame and image recognition.

"Freud was not only found to be very authoritative and well-known, but his image proved also to be highly recognizable and prototypical. The idea that simply "feeling like Freud" can affect our self-perception is powerful."

The study demonstrates that the vibrational energy we need to retrain our subconscious mind must be based in belief. The subjects "believed" Freud would have the answers they needed because he was an authority. What you believe becomes your reality because you make that belief real in your mind.

Your thoughts are powerful. Learning to create new thoughts that will move you in the right direction begins with the belief that this is possible and grows from there. The "virtual reality" in your subconscious is more than a computer image. It's real energy that can be trained to vibrate at a higher frequency, the frequency between the earthly plane and Divinity.

We Are Spiritual Beings Having a Human Experience

I've already discussed how we are made of energy, just like all things in the known universe, and modern physics has proven that energy cannot be created or destroyed. Given that, we can assume that what we are made of—energy—will go on "living" long after our human form is gone.

This is the animating force that gives us life. Call it energy or call it spirit. The bottom line is that our spirit is our direct connection to all things.

"You live in multi-dimensions of pure being, imagination, and physical body. So the real question is what domain you wish to live in. To me, the ideal life is lived on all levels of consciousness."

- Deepak Chopra, *The Book of Secrets: Unlocking the Hidden Dimensions of Your Life*

1. **The Body is the entire material structure and substance of an organism; the sum or physical part of man as distinguished from mind or spirit.**

   You live in a body, one which is vulnerable to external elements, one which can be physically pushed, pulled, and moved around. It takes a form which can be seen by the naked eye.

   It is a container and a transporter of organs, cells, systems, and individual members, all comprising this whole thing we call our body. A finger is just a finger, a heart is just a heart, and an ear is just an ear. But together they work synergistically for the good of the entire system, the body.

Your body also "contains" your mind and your spirit. These are the things which are a little more difficult to wrap your head around.

2. **The Mind is human consciousness manifested as thought, perception, or imagination and regarded as an aspect of reality.**

The mind is not a concept; it is measurably capable of luminescence. In physics, bioluminescence is the process by which energy is derived from non-thermal sources. We do not strike a match to our brain, or place a light bulb near it, or blow hot air onto it; the brain's energy and luminescence are that of its own making.

Science to date has not been able to separate the functionality of the brain from actual thought or imagination, but what can be measured on a spectrophotometer is the distribution of energy as seen in wavelengths. The energy is real, it's measurable, and it is inextricably part of the human body.

If you are a runner, you know that after a five-mile run, your body is warm or incalescent and is therefore incandescent—emitting visible or radiant light as a result of heat. Measuring or sensing the radiant heat and light of the human body is easily done using the proper instruments.

If you are an artist, you know that a color spectrum is a graphic representation of the refractive dispersion of light. These are real and measurable sciences that have traditionally been accepted by the general public.

If you accept that when you run, you get warm and like a light bulb that gets warm, gives off light measured in lumens or units of power, and that a color spectrum can be measured in terms of the dispersion of light, then you will understand that the mind's energy can be measured through its heat and its light.

3. **The Spirit is the animating force traditionally believed to be within living beings; the soul, intangible, and believed by some to be independent from the physical body in nature; generally regarded as immortal.**

   While the body is completely measurable and the mind is the newest horizon for studying the measurability and therefore the potential of humankind, the spirit or soul is intangible; we cannot reach it by any measurable standard or technology.

   Yet if you have ever been in love or felt compassion or a deep connection to a loved one, especially as experienced after the death of the loved one, you are aware of your essence, your spirit, your soul.

   Love cannot be seen or measured by science. Yet brainwaves have shown a significant difference in subjects who were tested after having watched a sad movie and a love story. The effects of love can be measured but not love itself, yet most of us would agree it exists.

   How then can we agree that something exists if we cannot sense it in the physical way, using the five physical senses?

How Science Explains the Existence of Spirit

Humans exist within the visible (to the human eye) portion of the electromagnetic spectrum. This spectrum is a measure of light calculated by the distance between light waves and how frequently they pass a certain point per second.

Above the visible portion of the spectrum, increasing in length and decreasing in frequency, are barely visible near infrared, microwaves, and various radio waves. On the other end, decreasing in length and increasing in frequency are ultraviolet, x-rays, and gamma rays.

Researchers, supported by electromagnetic measurements, distinguish eight major aspects of the energy network in humans, one of which is the aura, the fundamental energy shield emanating from and surrounding us. Could this be the Spirit? Or at least part of it?

The auric field functions as a protective buffer against external negative energy and can extend from 2-9 feet outward in every direction. It changes in color, brightness and size depending on your physical health, thoughts and feelings, and it can grow brighter and stronger with consistent healthy body/mind/spirit practices such as meditation and proper breathing.

What is the Human Biofield?

Humans are creatures of light. Human energy is light energy, equal to quantum energy, with dimensions within dimensions, all made of subatomic particles and all in an excited state vibrating at varying speeds. The energy biofield is the blueprint network that links all our aspects: cells, organs, DNA, meridians, nerve channels, and mental frequencies. It behaves like a superconductor transporting energy just like an electric grid.

The aura field consists of several layers and is an extension of the human biofield. It emanates from the form into the ether or space. Picture a dense spinning light rod, which is not solid but made of tiny particles of light, which runs vertically through your body. It extends out through the top of your head and out through the tail bone. As it spins, electrical sparks fly from it through nerve channels, blood, organs, and skin. What is revealed on the outside is the extension of that current known as the aura.

- It is seen as fluid and dynamic, able to exert influence over another living body.

- It contains polarities just like any electromagnetic field, but with a significant difference. With EMFs, opposites attract. In the auric field, like attracts like.

- It carries a charge and different frequencies.

- It is measurable and photographable using Kirlian photography.

- Like all energy, it is unbounded, a fact of physics.

While some scientists view the aura as subatomic particles or bio plasma, others suggest it is a negative mass that allows a shift between this world and another. Perhaps it is a combination of both.

Now Digg this: In earlier times, auras were believed to be miracles. Nearly 100 different cultures reference the human aura, each culture calling it by a different name: astral light, corona, luminous body, halo, ring, aureole, and others. This is indeed the spirit.

But there is nothing paranormal in the universe. Everything is energy vibrating at various rates of speed. And we, as humans, are part of that universal mastery. The energy that is left behind after the physical dies is the Spirit, now having ended this particular human experience.

Energy is neutral; it does not take up the body being happy or sad, greedy or generous, benevolent or malevolent. But what it experiences in this journey creates a veil to what it really is. It becomes what we make it by the power of our intention to mold it.

In this way, you are able to understand that, although you cannot touch the path or the intention for your desire, you can use the energy within you to create it, to make it appear for you, to make it real through the Decisions you make. It's all connected, and your mind is the vehicle upon which it will travel.

Once you 'get' this, you (your spirit) become free to define what happiness is to you. You can move forward making decisions, choosing what you want, and applying the power of your Spirit energy, through the vehicle of your mind, to get what you want to be, do and have. (I talk more about this in the chapter on Imagination).

But there are many reasons your Spirit can become polluted, and much of it has to do, once again, with what you've learned to believe about yourself. And this is important. You learned through your experiences to believe certain things, whether it's about yourself, your world, politics, other people, social behaviors, or anything else. We're not born with judgements, we learn them.

Understanding Control Dramas & Energy Parasites

With everything else you are trying to learn about yourself, here's something else that will have played a huge role in molding how your life may have unfolded and how you view your world: control dramas. As I have said, we're not born with judgements, we've learned them. Control dramas are something we learn early on, in childhood, and we use them to get what we want.

Understanding how control dramas work and what yours is will go a long way to explaining a lot about yourself, your family, your friends, how you react to others, and how this all plays together.

The struggle for power is characterized by a need for energy, and energy deficits are the main cause of interpersonal conflict. People use what is referred to as a control drama to fill up their energy stores at the expense of others. And some give up their energy willingly.

The control drama you've adopted has masked your authentic self behind a manipulative behavior that's used to get what you want from others. It's created a shield against the world and acts as a defense mechanism. Now you will learn to get what you want not from external energy, but from your own internal energy.

What are energy parasites?

An energy parasite is a person who is using a control drama on you for personal gain. Very early on, as children, we begin to lose some of our power. In order to gain it back, we learn to manipulate for energy either aggressively, by directly forcing people to pay attention to us, or passively, by playing on curiosity or sympathy. We play out certain dramas which are effective for drawing the attention or energy we need, and in doing so we begin the cycle of pain and suffering caused by being judgmental. Your spirit does not want to be judgmental. Spirit is pure love that has lost sight of its identity and purpose because of energy parasites—those people you've experienced who made you believe something about yourself that isn't true.

There are 4 types of energy parasites.

   Intimidator: An intimidator or bully may use physical or verbal force. Adults intimidate their children by hitting and yelling. Spouses intimidate with threats or bodily harm. Bosses who yell at employees are intimidators. Schoolyard bullies are intimidators. Gang leaders are intimidators. The intimidator is the gangster of energy parasites.

   Interrogator: An interrogator is a fault finder. This person always finds something wrong as a way of keeping someone else down. Nagging, nit-picking and constant questioning are favorite tools of interrogators. But the interrogator is only effective on someone who is willing to believe what is said about them, so this parasite must have a weak victim who is malleable and lacks confidence.

Aloof: This person acts mysterious, keeping to themselves in an attempt to force others to draw them out. Sulking is one of their tools. When asked "what's wrong?" this type will always tell you nothing is wrong, attempting to hold your attention.

Poor Me: This person always has a pitiable story. Nothing ever goes right for them. You believe they just need a shoulder to cry on, but this person is one of the most manipulative energy stealers because their play on your sympathy never ends.

As children, we're fighting to be heard; vying for position. The oldest always got in trouble for what the others did, so he might become an Interrogator, always making others feel it's their fault, laying blame before it can be laid on him.

The youngest might have been last in line for everything, so this child learned that with a few tears Mom or Dad would pick her up to comfort her. She gets the energy she needs by making others feel sorry for her.

Giving up your control drama takes courage and conscious effort because the subconscious mind has made you believe that this is how you can stay in power. But as an young adult or near-adult, you have your own power. You don't need to fight for it anymore.

Every time your control drama comes up, don't allow it to dominate how you react. It's just residual imprinting from your childhood, teens or young adult societal interactions.

Look for the following energy parasite symptoms in yourself and others:

- Blaming others for your situation

- Complaining, nagging or nit-picking

- Seeing things as unfair; feeling sorry for yourself

- Using derogatory language or raising your voice to intimidate someone; bullying

- Not opening up with your feelings; remaining aloof

Any resistance to letting go of your control drama is directly related to your fears, which have become the point of power for everything you do. What you fear–loss, hurt, embarrassment, loneliness, humiliation, rejection–is what controls you. If you see a pattern either now or in your past, you will see that you have been the obstacle all along.

Control dramas require an audience. When you understand that all the energy is yours, there will be no need for one.

- Express yourself without expectation or the need for validation.

- Don't react; slow down your interactions with others

- Allow others to fill up with energy by giving them time and space to speak

- Become a non-judgmental audience

Once you understand the struggle, you can begin to break free. Eventually the motives and actions of energy thieves will become transparent and won't have any effect on you. And you'll begin to realize that you don't need to steal energy from others. There will be no struggle because of your intention to keep your own energy.

Never give your power to anyone outside of yourself. Instead, give your devotion and loyalty to the inherent power within each of us, that which is created by the Universe, the God within you, and of which we all have an equal measure. The Divine Spirit within you knows all you need to know. You just need to learn to access that knowledge.

What is Self-Worth & Value?

It's what every person needs to be productive. Whose self-worth and value do we increase by writing down and accomplishing goals on a daily basis? We increase our own.

We are giving ourselves exactly what it takes to feel wonderful. That feeling of accomplishment increases our self-worth and value and makes us feel better about ourselves as well as feeling better about those around us.

What kind of an attitude do you have about your self-worth?

By having daily goals and Mind Maps, fulfilling them and checking the Map off, you are force-feeding yourself with self-worth and value. That self-worth and value will develop a great attitude in you. (I'll talk more about this in Chapter 7: The 5th Power: G: Go! The Power of Going).

The three percent of people who control the world all have a great attitude about themselves and their world. So what you're actually doing is creating a high and injecting yourself in the arm every day. That's where your attitude comes from. The attitude doesn't come from the outside world. It comes from you showing yourself over and over again how good you are.

In my book, I AM, I talk about a powerful exercise using binaural beats every morning. This is where you listen to the beats and state to yourself who you are. It's not about saying I want to be this or that type of person. It's about saying I AM this person.

Accomplish something—anything—that will bring you closer to your long term goals - every day. Remember, this is the shot in the arm that will keep you going.

Inspiration is active, not passive. Don't wait around for some muse to strike making you its lucky recipient. Be someone who participates in the power of your own accomplishments—the accomplishments that precede you and that now empower and inspire you to keep moving forward. Remain active in discovering what works to your success and in applying those lessons to your own talents.

Remember, your view of your failures, your fear of more failure, and your lack of placing importance on whatever successes you've had up to this point are what have been holding you back. This is where you were not aware of your thoughts and so you did not evaluate them or correct them. By allowing others to design your present, you've allowed them to create what will ultimately be your future.

Now it's time for you to take control of your own life through your own thoughts and actions, not those of the outside world.

Can You DIGG It? I knew that you could!

5.

THE THIRD POWER:
D: THE POWER OF DECISION

*"Once you make a decision, the Universe conspires
to make it happen."*

- Ralph Waldo Emerson

As humans—spiritual beings having a human experience—the Universe has blessed us with the power to decide who we want to be, what we want to do and what we want to have. We have the power of choice and reasoning. Make the decision to be Healthy, Wealthy, Successful, and Happy. (In my second book, I Am, I show you the steps to do that).

In an article by the Tlex Institute[21] citing a study by the National Science Foundation, the human mind is capable of 60,000 or more thoughts per day, or about forty-one thoughts per minute. But they say 95% of those thoughts are repetitive and about 80% are negative. But not all repetitive thoughts are bad. If you make a decision and a plan, and then focus on that, you will be thinking about it often. These are repetitive thoughts that are beneficial.

So think about thinking—in other words, be aware of your thoughts—and who this person is who is doing all this thinking. Who are you and who do you want to be? Do your thoughts align with your intentions? You cannot empty your mind of all thoughts because awareness is not empty. You will always be thinking about something, so why not focus on what you want?

You Know More Than You Think You Know

"It's in your moments of decision that your destiny is shaped."

- Tony Robbins

We need constant vigilance to stay on top of our experiences and our awareness. Emotions and feelings come into play and these can often be difficult to control. We all have a breaking point— triggers, and buttons that can be pushed. So it's not necessarily a matter of avoiding feeling something, it's a matter of understanding why you have certain triggers. What is the hidden meaning behind them? What underlies your sense of guilt, pain, sorrow, or anger? This was your objective in making your three Maps.

As you become more objectively aware or your reactions and behaviors, you may have a sudden sense that your actions up to now were not being controlled by you. If you were living a gilded life, a life that was not authentically you, the world was using you for its own ends.

But when you improve your powers of observation and are able to be aware of each moment, you will sense that decision making has become easier.

You may even discover your life's purpose. You may discover you've just been playing along for most of your life, and you may begin to experience a feeling of complete focus.

But you must be willing to let go of your past habits of thought and subjective perception. That doesn't mean there won't be obstacles. But you might discover that sometimes the obstacle is the path. Every decision can lead to a lesson. Failure can be success because you will have learned something. And creativity will open your vision.

With every new decision you make, now backed by clarity of thought and control over your emotions, you will be creating a new philosophy of your own, and this is what will govern your attitude and determine your actions.

If your thoughts, beliefs, and decisions have gotten you to where you are today, are you happy? If you're answer is no, then changing what you believe and the way you make decisions will get you somewhere else tomorrow. Don't think small; dream big and reach for what you want.

Seek to understand rather than to change.

"Be willing to make decisions. That's the most important quality in a good leader. Don't fall victim to what I call the 'ready-aim-aim-aim' syndrome. You must be willing to fire." (T. Boone Pickens)

By giving up the struggle to change your life, you will experience things getting better because you will be more observant of how things happen. You will begin to understand how reactions often take you down a wrong path. Stop being a stranger to yourself. Let yourself emerge and be the experiencer who understands that it is your awareness that makes things what they are. No one else will see the significance of what you experience, but it will lead to the perfect unity of thoughts what will enable you to be confident in your decision-making.

There are four components to the ultimate Power of Decision:

1. **Feeling:** Understand why things happen.

2. **Thinking:** Direct your thinking to all that is positive; detach yourself from thinking about negative outcomes.

3. **Action:** You must take the necessary steps and guide your own actions. This includes a decision to be dedicated to your goal.

4. **Being:** You will then just allow unity of thought (a focus on what you want to be, do, and have) to guide you because you are now living in complete awareness of thoughts and your behavior. Your Power of Decision is grounded in the reality that you have created for yourself.

Once you understand how emotions affect your reactions, and you've identified your authentic self, every decision you make will come from a place of clarity.

What you need to do is simply say, "What has happened in the past happened [because of this reason]. Now I want the main influence in my life to go [in this direction], a direction of my own choosing." It will start you on the path to changing your perception of why things happened as they did and how they can no longer inform your actions or reactions.

Your point of power will then come from your changed perception. Every thought has only the meaning you give it, so incidents that once negatively informed your reactions to life will now be positively created by you.

Your mind is your salvation. There are infinite opportunities for you to create, and by declaring your intention to move in a certain direction, you call upon all the possibilities that exist, thereby increasing probability in your favor.

I'm not a person who believes in coincidences. What I do believe is that there is an appointed time and place for everything that happens in our lives. That's not to say that life is a straight line. For most of us, it's not. The decisions you make determine your outcome, and that outcome may show up tomorrow or ten years from now. Let me put that another way. The decisions you make and the actions you take today determine the results that will at some point show up in your life. But don't start thinking too much about all the mistakes you've made. Look at them and learn from them, then move on to correct them.

Some mistakes can't be corrected, but you can begin today to make a better tomorrow. Most mistakes, however, can be turned around simply by recognizing and understanding where you went wrong and choosing to make a course correction. Remember that word choose, because everything you do is a choice.

It's All About Learned Responses

"Life is the sum of all your choices."

- Albert Camus

You know those overnight successes? Their success started when they made the decision to follow a certain path and devoted ever increasing amounts of energy toward what they wanted to see happen. They took control, implemented strategies, and remained flexible so they could make course corrections along the way. The same holds true for those lifelong failures. They, too, followed a certain path, putting all their energy into negative beliefs, whether they were aware of it or not.

But the one thing all successful people have in common regardless of their pursuit is they don't give up. They believe they can do something, they put their faith to work and they keep moving.

They make choices and they make decisions based on what they believe to be possible. What you believe is possible will make all the difference. In fact, if you believe something is not possible, you have also made a choice. Even by not making any decision at all, you have made a decision and the world will take its toll on you whether you are aware of it or not.

So stop asking yourself, "Why did this happen to me?" Just make the decision to embrace the belief that something else is possible for you. If you do not remove the old video tape that keeps playing in your mind and replace it with something new, you will never be able to fulfill the vision you have for yourself.

The fact that you have a vision for yourself is a step in the right direction. You've recognized something and given it credence. Focus on that.

It's no mistake that you have this book in your hands. You are positioning yourself for success by beginning a strategy. You've made a decision. The determination with which you push forward toward your future or push away from an unsatisfying past will automatically be the boost you need to get you through all the things that might appear to be obstacles.

This brings me to another issue which I have found to be true among those who are not willing or able to recognize the fact that they have become stagnate. They are not receptive to hearing something new, listening to advice or searching out new opportunities or avenues for growth. They simply prefer to live with their dream, never actually taking the actions necessary to make it manifest. There's nothing wrong with watching TV all day if that's what you truly want, but you cannot expect to become better at anything if you don't get off the couch and practice.

And that applies to life on the field and off. In the classroom and outside of it. It's really what life is all about. Practice. What you do in practice is what your life will become.

Stay curious. Don't worry and don't accept labels such as loser, failure or dysfunctional. In everything you do, you should gain a new awareness that can support your current goals. If something doesn't pan out the way you expected it to, ask yourself the following questions:

- What happened along the way that might have caused this result?

- How can I improve on the process to get better results?

- What is the most practical way I can improve my plan?

- Where can I expand my knowledge base regarding this project or goal?

- Did I fail to do something that was required of me?

- Can I spot any missing components that might have helped?

- Can I look at this differently?

It's completely understandable that we get locked into a pattern of our peers. Pack mentality is common among teens. It's a time when we're searching for an identity, and the pack gives us that identity. We want to be validated and accepted. But there is no law in the universe that says you must stay locked where you are, that you must continue to do things the same way all the time. You are the one who determines what will work for you. Change can be a bit scary, but staying where you are, if you're not happy, is even worse.

Track a new path and allow doors to open for you by seeking out new resources. Take a different class or attend a seminar, seek out experts, find a mentor, read a book on the subject of your interest, learn something new. Each of these can lead you to an opportunity that might improve your chances of successfully completing your goal.

The possibility of failure is a great motivator to make us work harder. Most athletes understand this. Get out on that court or field, practice your swings or throws or kicks, perfect your stance, know your strategy; all of these things are decisions athletes make so they won't fail during a game. That doesn't mean it doesn't happen. We can't account for every move during a game, but the decisions you make go a long way to making sure you get close, even if it's not a 100% win.

Every phase of your life, every action you take and every experience you encounter are just stepping stones to your ultimate understanding of yourself. And the more you understand your own motivations, why you have been doing things a certain way, why you've made certain decisions, and ultimately how you see yourself and your life, the greater chance you will have at mastering your life.

The Importance of Knowing Your Why?

"Nothing gives a person inner wholeness and peace like a distinct understanding of where they are going."

- Thomas Oppong

In the exercise I gave you in Chapter 4: The 2nd Power: YOU: The Power of Identity, you discovered something about yourself, maybe a lot. You uncovered some of the reasons you react, behave, and believe the way you do. Now you're going to figure out why you want what you want. What is your main motivation? What does Loving Life mean to you? (You can experiment with this notion of how you would like to see yourself by using the Guided Visualization I've outlined for you in Appendix III and then building a Mind Map.)

You probably get out of bed every day reluctant to go to school or work. You have no motivation to do either and find little reward in going through the motions to fulfill someone else's vision; some institutional journey that fills up your day without imparting any benefit other than a small paycheck or not being thrown out of school.

You may think you know what you want, but you veer off the track often, distracted by friends or family obligations.

But getting to your "why", your main motivation, is the only way you'll be able to stay on track and get to your success.

Ikigai is a Japanese word that translates as "reason for being" or "reason to live". Your reason for living will be something that you feel deep within you; something that makes you feel alive and worthwhile. If it's football, if that's what you live for, this is your "why" for staying in school and getting good grades. If you're motivated by money, this is your "why" for staying with a good job, continuing to learn, or coming up with an innovative idea that will make you more money. If you're creative, inventing something may be your "why". You can quite possibly just love doing something. Why do you want to do something? Because you love doing it. It brings you joy.

There are four different reasons a person doesn't achieve something they want to achieve, even if they're gifted with great talent.

1. **They don't believe it can be done.** If you don't believe it can be done, you're never going to act on it, and that takes in a lot of people. These people often have a victim mentality; they believe themselves to be victims of their environment, their society, their jobs, their parents. They're really victims of their own thinking.

2. **They don't believe they can do it.** This is in contrast to number one, where they don't believe it can be done. This has to do with you doing it. You don't believe you can do it. Your habits or disciplines aren't there; they're way down at the bottom or you're priorities Map; you're just not willing to do the work.

3. **They don't have a powerful enough 'why'.** They're not drawn to or driven by anything. They haven't labeled why they have to do something; why they're compelled to do something.

4. **They don't know the 'how'.** They might believe that it can be done and they have a powerful why, but they don't know how to do it, how to get from point A to point B.

I've talked a lot about the Power of Beliefs. Once you begin to believe something is possible and you believe you can do it, and you know why you want to do it, the how will follow, generally showing up in your life on its own.

Here's what you need to do to discover your why. This will bring you clarity and keep you focused on your goals. It will keep the passion in your pursuits and give you the resilience to withstand setbacks.

- Think about the activities that made you forget about time. You were lost in your activity and time passed without you noticing how long you were at it. You were in the zone. You were experiencing flow. You were energized, not drained. Time flew by.

- Think about the things you liked doing as a kid. We tend to forget those things because societal pressures take them away from us. Look for patterns that repeat themselves.

- Don't just think about the things that can bring you monetary rewards.

- Think about what you would do even if you were not getting paid, or if you looked foolish doing it, but you still are willing to do it because it's something you love.

- What are your talents? Do people ask you for help or advice in certain areas?

- What would you do if you only had a short time, say a year, to live? How you want to spend that time if you weren't concerned about money, resources or other limitations?

- Have you ever been willing to go the extra mile at something?

- If someone asked you to teach a child something, what would that be?

- What would you do if you knew you couldn't fail?

You can think about your why as your calling in life. It's your core motivation and will be what defines you. If you're feeling overwhelmed or frustrated, you're likely living to fulfill someone else's why and are not in alignment with your unique purpose.

What are your core beliefs or values? This is your code of conduct and should also be alignment with your why.

Your strengths are your natural abilities, talents, and both technical and life skills.

What you're most passionate about is the thing that you just can't get enough of. You want to spend endless hours doing it, and your friends and family might even consider you a guru or "expert" on the subject.

Why are you drawn to something? What are your most focused thoughts? What do you think about all day?

So, using football as an example, you thought football was going to be your life. You played in high school and college, but you got banged in the knee and never fully recovered. Your football career is over. Forever. What do you do?

You find another why.

Get it out of your head that you will no longer be able to play ball. Can you coach? What would be the most ideal work day for you now? Can you go back to school and learn to become a physical therapist? A sports therapist?

What drew you to football in the first place? Was it the glory and attention? The comradery? The feeling of belonging to some-thing bigger than yourself?

These are all things you can get from other careers. What is the emotional motivation behind any of your choices?

- What can you get excited about seeing yourself doing?

- What would feel effortless to you?

- What are you curious about?

- What would give you a sense of value, self-esteem, and fulfillment?

- Is there something you can't stop thinking about?

- What's most important about…?

In my book, I AM, I talk about another one of my mentors, and now friend, Mr. Joe Stumpf, who devised this strategy he calls the Ultimate Scenario for determining your "why".

In short, we must decide who we want to be before we can do anything else. Think about someone who is currently doing something you would love to do.

- How is that person being?

- How is that person's "Being" different from yours?

- What do you need to adjust to be more like that person?

- What can you do to start having what that person has?

The idea is to use that person as a role model and emulate the action steps they took to get where they are.

If you were in an Ultimate Scenario session with Joe Stumpf, you would be asked a series of thought-provoking questions. Here's what the scenario looks like. We'll use buying a home as the example. So the first question is "What's important about buying a home to you?

This is the most important dialogue in the series, and you will do most of the talking. Joe would ask you further questions and listen to your answers.

Please DIGG This!

Think of something that you would like to be, do or have? _____

What is most important about (Your Answer) to you? _____

What is most important about (Your Answer) to you? _____

What is most important about (Your Answer) to you? _____

What is most important about (Your Answer) to you? _____

What is most important about (Your Answer) to you? _____

What is most important about (Your Answer) to you? _____

Joe says we must ask ourselves this same question at least six times to get to your real why. To get to the emotional reason for doing something.

Each of Joe's Ultimate Scenario questions would be designed so that you can explore your inner mind more deeply and get at the root of what you want and what might be holding you back. This is something you can do with your Mind Map, something I can help you with.

This is the only way to hone in on your best path to success. Can You DIGG It? I knew that you could.

Define What Success Means to You

How much money do you want to have? Is it respect or recognition that's most important? Maybe a promotion? Or do you simply want to be able to call your own shots, to be your own boss? Write down what success means to you personally, how you define it in words, not just in a vision of a big house or pool or car, although these can be part of your success story, Give it life. This goes back to seeing the vision of yourself being or doing what you want to be or do. You can't set a goal or make corrections to what you're thinking if you don't know what you want to think about! You need to discover and define what you want.

Stop playing the dutiful daughter or son or husband or mother or secretary or shopkeeper. These roles were created for you. Create a new role for yourself in your definition of success. Be your own superstar.

Don't be too hard on yourself.

Comparing yourself to others is the worst thing you can do. It will only serve to demoralize you unless you have emotions of steel. Never play the 'poor me' card and feel sorry for yourself. And don't blame others for any of it. Forget about everything that happened up to this point and focus on the goal you're trying to achieve, the career you're trying to create or the sale you're trying to close. You can't make up for lost time, so simply look to the future. Remember: what got you here were the thoughts you gave power to. Getting where you want to be will take only changing that.

"Watch your thoughts, they become words; watch your words, they become actions; watch your actions, they become habits; watch your habits, they become character; watch your character, it becomes your destiny." (Frank Outlaw)

Know the difference between what's under your control and what isn't; the difference between someone else's ideas of success and your own. What's right for them may not be right for you.

If you do feel as though you can't make the break because you're still fearful of losing your security, try volunteering to help with assignments outside of your current job description. Demonstrate to your company and to yourself that you have abilities beyond what's believed. Learn and grow.

You can spend years of your life waiting for the right moment and the right circumstance. Decide what it is you want then go about setting goals to make that happen. Sometimes making the break is the only option.

Trust yourself and your instincts. Doors will open for you but only if you leave a space for that to happen.

Align Your Goals for Success

Each of us has had times in our lives when everything seems to flow seamlessly, when we don't really have to do anything to make something go our way and everyone in our circle seems to be cooperative.

And then there are times when it feels as though everything we attempt is a struggle, nothing seems to go right and we're butting heads at every turn. In those moments, it's resistance that's causing things to feel like a struggle. When it seems as though nothing is going your way, it might be that you're not paying attention to subtle clues that could turn things in your favor.

If you think about and recognize the people in your life, past and current, who have changed you in some way, made some significant contribution to your life, who have made a difference, know that it was always a two way street. You made a difference to them as well. The acts of giving and receiving are both impactful. Because someone gave to you, you gave meaning to their act of giving. You allowed yourself to receive. So in that moment, you also gave.

Had you not been open to receiving, you would have closed the pathway between yourself and the giver. You would have denied them the experience of giving and you both would have lost whatever it was that was intended for that moment.

How is your mental framework keeping you from reaching your goals?

There are numerous obstacles or types of resistance that can be keeping you from opening pathways for success. And one path or open doorway will always lead to another, Being open, dropping resistance and letting go of trying to control how things will happen, will lead you down a path that can show you something you may not anticipate or couldn't possibly have planned for.

Having a plan is good, but trying to allow for every situation is almost impossible. Be flexible.

These are some common types of resistance that block us from reaching our goals and indicate that you're trying to control how things will happen.

- **Setting goals too high** - Having unrealistic goals will render you helpless in reaching them. Break goals into manageable bits where you can see the end result in a shorter amount of time. Measure your goal against a time frame but be flexible if something goes wrong.

- **Procrastination** – Having mixed emotions about what it is you want will keep you from moving forward. Procrastination can stem from outright laziness, lack of preparation, fear of failing, insecurity about your abilities, a lack of awareness about your options, or feeling overwhelmed and not knowing how to get started. Even economic limitations shouldn't keep you from taking action. Find some small bit you can afford to do and let the rest fall into place. Don't try to figure it all out at once.

- **Worrying about things that are out of your control** – There's only so much we can control in life. Spending time worrying about those things will debilitate you and stop you from moving forward. Worry is a time waster. If you can't fix it, leave it.

- **Lack of preparation** - Be prepared, getting some training and honing your skills should all be part of your plan. When opportunity strikes, you'll be able to take advantage of it. If you hit a wall, find a work-around but don't let it stop you. Be specific about what you want to achieve and make sure the steps you take are relevant to the end result.

- **Mental framework** – What you believe you can do is all that you can do. If you hold onto mental roadblocks, thinking you can't do something, that's exactly what you'll achieve. Nothing.

- **Not knowing what you want** - Sitting on the fence being unable to make a decision is a form of fear and procrastination. Decide what you want, what you want to achieve and what it will take to make it to the point where you feel you've succeeded in that endeavor. Make a Mind Map of what you will need and how you'll go about getting to the end, visualize the end and how it will look, then make a total commitment. You may need to revisit the previous chapter. Or you can sign up for my free Decision Mind Mapping webinar at johndiggs.com

- **Not being open to meaningful coincidence** – There are forces greater than ourselves at work. Listen to what others have to offer and learn from that. You may find some comment or idea that can help you.

But in order for any of this to work, you must first learn to release negativity. It can keep you focused on what you can't do rather than what you can do. It will illuminate all the irritating aspects and keep you from seeing new things. And it will close your mind as a means of protection.

Releasing negativity will help you develop a conscious effort toward your intention; whatever it is you want to achieve.

The consciousness to align yourself with what you want requires you to take control of your habits so you can clearly see your desires and make them happen. The more these practices become habit, imprinting themselves in your brain, the better you'll get at bringing anything that's right for you to have.

Remain alert and responsive to the people and coincidences in your life - not only those new coincidences but all the important people who currently surround you - friends, family, co-workers. Anyone close to you very likely has something to show you that will move you forward in your evolutionary process.

Doubt, negativity, resentment, and anger can lead to illness and mutation within cells. Don't focus on the past or on the future. Being fully present means you must feel BlessednGrateful™ now; you must be at peace with your fears and all your negative thoughts and feelings now, in the present. In that way, you will limit your regret in the future. Today will be your past, so every thought you have, what you're grateful for now, the peace you create with your environment now will become what you will experience later, in the future.

Stepping away from them and releasing the energy you've given them will allow you to give that energy to new imprints. You'll gain insight because you've opened up 'space', making room for new ideas to come in.

Spend 80% of your time focused on where you're going, where you want to go, and the other 20% on finding solutions. This is how you'll bring excitement to your life. Take advantage of every opportunity that presents itself if it's going to bring you closer to your goal. If an opportunity appears in your life and it's in alignment with your goals, don't be lazy. If an occasion arises, follow up on it. If someone invites you to an event and it's related to the field you want to get into, go to it even if you can't see the benefits up front.

And when you feel doubt creeping in, think about these six criteria for pushing through successfully:

- Don't underestimate yourself
- Don't focus on your shortcomings

- Don't justify your fear

- Be your authentic self

- Take both criticism and praise gracefully

- Remember why you're there

The Thought Police

Thought patterns can be broken down into four categories which collectively cover just about everything in our lives. These are the Thought Police:

- Health: includes fitness, weight loss, disease, physical self-image

- Dollars: includes investments, savings, anything relating to money

- Business: includes career, job, school

- Relationships: includes family, friends, relatives, associates

Each time you reach for success in any area, the Thought Police come in and place restrictions, telling you that you can't have that.

The Law of Abundance states that there is an unlimited amount of everything for everyone. There is no lack. It will never run out. When you align yourself with this principle, your belief that there just isn't enough to go around will fade.

These things are trying to reach you, but because of your limited world view, you are not allowing yourself to receive. You may be telling yourself that you really want something, but your subconscious is remembering all the times you didn't get it, whatever it is. It replays those same thoughts and experiences over and over. The magic is you can substitute new thoughts and experiences that will work in the same way; thoughts of success and experiences that the mind thinks are real even though they haven't actually happened yet.

Remember, where you focus your attention is what you will attract, but if you've left the wall of the past in place, what you attract won't be able to get through. You must believe you deserve it. A mistake is only a mistake if you let it be one; if you stay fixated on it and believe it to be so. Once you become aware of this simple fact, you will begin to question everything. You will see the significance of everything and you will be the one to decide which of these things is worth your attention. When you get answers, they will always bring more questions.

The Thought Police are working for you – or against you – whether you realize it or not. You don't believe there's enough to go around. You don't believe you're capable of losing the weight and keeping it off this time. You don't believe you can land that client or close that sale. You don't believe you're pretty enough, smart enough, talented enough, lucky enough to deserve the privilege of the few who 'have it all'. This is referred to as a scarcity mindset. If you're still having a problem with changing your beliefs about who you are and what you deserve, please revisit Chapter 2: The Power of Beliefs.

But the Laws work equally for everyone.

You haven't yet recognized that by not focusing your energy and consciousness on what you want to become, you became the random manifestation of all the energy that you've experienced, which has developed into your current perspective. You have subconsciously put out to the world everything you believe about the way things are, that there is lack, not enough to go around, and this is what you've received. Change what you put out and you will change what you get back.

You will begin to say, "Oh, I'd like to do that," instead of, "I can't do that."

Can You DIGG It? I knew that you could!

6.

THE FOURTH POWER: I: THE POWER OF IMAGINATION

"Trust that little voice in your head that says, "Wouldn't it be interesting if..." and then do it."

- Duane Michals

The human mind is all imagination. Every thought that ever occurred was imagined by someone. But most thoughts are repetitive. They provide no inspiration. They are nothing more than a tape playing itself over and over again.

The Point of Power

Nothing exists outside of this moment. I know that's hard to wrap your head around. But nothing ever happened in the past or in the future. Every moment happened at the moment it happened and each moment was in the present. No matter what happens in life, it's always in the present moment. This is where inspiration shows itself, and it's only in the present moment that you will be able to guide your actions. But you must be aware of what's happening, really aware, hyper-aware, as though everything is moving in slow motion.

That moment is known as the Point of Power. The past and the future have no realities of their own. They are mirror images of your thoughts and they exist now - in the present. Understand that any unhappiness you experience is caused by denial of the present and attachment to the past and the future.

It's impossible to have a problem when you're living in the present moment - when you're present. You either deal with the situation or you accept it. It's only remains a problem if you dwell on it without the intention to take action now.

What is Your Mind-Set?

Here's something I found very interesting. A study done by a Stanford University psychology professor offers some startling insight.

Students were given intricate puzzles and were observed while in the process of putting the puzzles together. Some students were concerned with putting the puzzle together quickly while others were soon defeated.

Some saw the puzzle as a challenge. They were excited by the puzzles they had trouble with and rather than being defeated, became more determined.

Rather than being intimidated, they didn't see this as failing, but instead actually viewed the challenge as a learning experience. They had the mindset that they could do it. They just knew they could do it.

This is important to note. The fixed mindset believes that talent, natural gifts, IQs, and SATs will get them far in life. If this were indeed the case, then the opposite would also be true. Any lack of talent or "smarts" would limit how far you can go in life.

So you see how this is all tied to only what you believe you're good at.

You're capable of far more than you might ever imagine, but stretching yourself beyond your comfort zone is the only way to grow. You can always learn new skills that will give you new abilities to succeed.

Unlocking One of the Mysteries of the Mind

The average human brain only weighs about 3 pounds and is remarkable in its complexity. Some believe it is the seat of the mind while others believe the mind is in the subtle body, the network of energy we emit as living creatures.

Whichever you believe, the mind controls and dictates all our thoughts, deeds, and reactions. But it essentially started as a blank slate and your mind can go as far back as the beginning of humankind as we know it.

Ninety percent of what we do is done unconsciously. Consider this:

Hwo cna yuo raed tihs atricle atbou teh brian?

Most people can read that sentence without giving it much thought because the brain has perceived the words as they should be. It has instantly unscrambled each word at the time it is read because it has seen the words before.

According to Matt James, Ph. D. (Psychology Today), the unconscious mind has the following characteristics:

1. **It acts like a child:** The unconscious mind needs very clear and detailed directions. It takes things literally. For example, if your favorite saying is "cleaning is a pain in the rear", you may begin to experience pains in the posterior.

    Key: Give your mind precise, affirmative, literal directives.

2. **Communicates through emotions and symbols:** Whether something is dangerous or joyful, it will attract your attention through an emotion (fear or happiness), regardless of whether it's a valid response or not. That will depend on your subjective experience.

    Key: Learn to recognize which events are valid in causing fear, anger, joy, or any other emotion. Don't simply react.

3. **Deals only with positives:** So any negative words you might utter as a way of succeeding or moving forward are ignored by the unconscious mind. Statements such as "I don't want to overeat" will be perceived as "overeat". Your mind will create a picture of you overeating.

    Key: Make positive statements such as "I eat well and just enough to be healthy."

4. **Makes associations and learns quickly:** This is vital to survival and includes your physical body as well as your emotional condition. The unconscious mind must instantly assess a situation and is always vigilant so it can alert and protect you.

    On the down side, it remembers almost too well. So if you forgot your lines in the school play, anything associated with being in front of an audience might make you nervous and anxious throughout your life.

The up side is you can tap into this stored information regarding your feelings and your body to determine your needs.

Key: Use reinforcement and behavior modification techniques to change your perception of negative experiences and rid yourself of unwarranted fears.

5. **Stores and organizes memories:** It determines which experiential memories to bring to the surface and which to supress in order to protect you.

   Key: Use meditation and relaxation to open your mind so it will release unresolved trauma or other aspects of your past you may be consciously unaware of.

How Does the Mind Gather Information?

The only way for us to experience anything is through the five senses. This is how the mind gets information. We must use these senses to breathe life into our imagination; to inspire it.

In order to successfully spark the imagination, we can engage dozens of sub-modalities while we're imagining. These can include visual, auditory, and kinesthetic senses. The more in tune we are with our senses, the more and better quality information we'll receive from the outside world.

Why is this important? Having the right information increases our chances of making the right decisions in any situation. This all goes back to The Power of Decision, but it starts with sensory input and using The Power of Imagination.

There is a small catch, however.

From the day you were born, memories began to be stored. After that, perception, cognition, and discernment were used by the unconscious mind to simulate a reality. When you have an experience, it fills in details based on past experiences.

But sometimes it gets a 'false reading'. The mind can misinterpret anything based on our own filters. These perspective filters are a product of our experience. So, for example, if you were bitten by a dog as a child, you may be fearful of all dogs. Now your son wants a dog of his own. Your experiential filter might prevent you from choosing the right dog or any dog at all. If you missed your lines in the high school play 10 years ago, it will tell you this is the reality of what's going to happen next time you get on a stage.

This goes back to the Power of Beliefs. Here's where that small catch comes in. You must clear the filters that are negatively influencing your life first before you can move on to effectively using sensory input to correctly seed your imagination.

Submodalities & Perspective Filters

The word submodality refers to any of the various qualities of a particular sense. So if we're talking about the sense of sight, we're going to look at anything that pertains to the quality of sight: clarity, color, and distance, for example. If we can change one or some of these qualities, it will have an impact on our memory.

In tangible application, if eyesight is poor, what we read may not make a great imprint on the brain. If glasses were prescribed to improve eyesight, reading becomes easier and therefore makes a greater imprint on the brain and memory.

Applying this to how the subconscious mind behaves, if we can change the images that are negatively impacting us, we change that memory. We can mentally change the color of a fire, for example, something that affected us psychologically, to grey rather than red and gold. We can push that image farther away in the scene that replays in our memory. We can lower any sounds or negative voices associated with that incident. All of these changes will affect how we feel about that memory.

What we take in from the outside world is collected in our memory. If we can explore how our senses take in this information, how it impacts us, and how we react to it personally, on an individual basis, we can get the right raw information and use our imagination correctly to create great outcomes.

Michael Beale is a neuro-linguistic programming (NLP) trainer and coach trainer who runs master classes at The Henley Business School. He's also a John Grinder[22] (co-founder of NLP) NLP coach and 'new code' practitioner.

New code NLP is described as having evolved from the classic code NLP by incorporating unconscious processes to stimulate outcomes that may not have been reached by dominant left brain logic, and which offers maximum choice in an individual's life.[22]

Michael Beale[23] offers us this list of submodalities:

Visual

- Association (associated or dissociated)

- Size (large or small)

- Motion (still or moving, slideshow or movie)

- Colour (colour or black and white)

- Brightness (bright or dark)

- Distance (near or far)

- Focus (focused or unfocused)

- Clarity (clear or fuzzy)

- Location (top, bottom, left, or right)
- Depth (2D or 3D)
- Frame (framed or panoramic)
- Number of images

Auditory

- Location (mono, stereo, surround)
- Tonality (flat or engaging)
- Tempo (slow or fast)
- Pitch (high or low)
- Pace (fast or slow)
- Intensity (intense or soft)
- Clarity (clear or fuzzy)
- Volume (loud or soft)
- Rhythm (regular or irregular)

Kinesthetic

- Location (Where do you feel it?)
- Vibration (Is it still or pulsing?)
- Movement (Is it still or moving? If it's moving trace the movement with your hands.)
- Pressure (Is there any pressure? If so, is it light or intense?)
- Shape (What shape is it?)
- Size (How big is it?)
- Temperature (Does it have a temperature? Is it warm or cool, or something else?)

- Direction (Does it have a direction? If so describe it)

- Steady or intermittent (Is it steady or intermittent?)

- Taste/Smell (Sweet, Sour, Aroma, Fragrance, Salt, Sweet, Essence, Pungency)

So you can see how many options you have for powering your imagination.

It is reported that Michael Jordan, one of the greatest basketball players of all time, used his power of imagination every night before a basketball game. While lying in bed he would play the whole game in his mind. He said he felt the coolness of the arena, heard shoes squeak on the floor, felt sweat on his face, felt the connection he had with the ball. He vividly imagined himself making the game-winning shot with seconds on the clock a thousand times. Which explains why he was so calm, cool and collected in those moments when they actually happened. Because he had seen it already, he knew what was going to happen. And it did!

In my book, I AM, I use this technique throughout. I also discuss the use of binaural beats. This is how I reframed my vision for myself and arrived at my current state of happiness and success.

(In Appendix III: Guided Visualization you will learn how to apply these submodalities in a sample guided visualization, which you can then use to power your own visualization, applying it to your individual desires.)

You have the conscious power to change your memory perception. Unlocking the unconscious mind is about manipulating where your attention goes and how, specifically, you want to direct it.

Walter Mischel, Ph.D., professor of psychology at Columbia University, said:

"The conception of willpower as a stoic thing, where you essentially will it and make it happen, is a terrific way to have resolutions that don't work out. You have to in some way engage the environment. The only thing you can do is change your perception, and change where you put your attention."[24]

Whether you're able to control your outcomes and decisions or not, it's always good to know how things work.

You can tap into your unconscious mind by opening up the creative process. Paint, draw, sing, dance; express yourself creatively.

Get in the habit of visualizing your desired outcomes, and this process can include your attitude, thoughts, reactions, and how you want a conversation to go.

Always use positive speech and thinking. In this way you affirm a consistency in keeping with what you want to be or achieve.

So being mindful of everything you say and how you allow situations to affect you, focusing on what you're doing right now, and generally become more engaged in the process of consciousness will help you unlock the secrets your unconscious mind is holding.

You've literally created the mind that directs you. Knowing this, you can make it do, remember, and point you in a direction of your choosing.

Imagine yourself successfully experiencing what you have decided for yourself.

We've all had moments of genius, where an idea neatly flows into implementation and successful completion, where we become completely absorbed in a task or project. Creative ideas come through sometimes without planning and everything seems to happen in slow motion. This is common among artists, musicians, dancers, writers, speakers, and some athletes such as skiers and footballers.

Unfortunately, we can't be in a flow state all the time. If we were, our brains would not be able to make evaluations and decisions, solve problems or analyze information. Many artistic types who spend much of their time in flow don't see the value of managing the rest of their life. Grooming and household chores are mundane and tedious to them and anything to do with the business end of their endeavors is lost.

The prefrontal cortex governs problem solving, data collection, pattern recognition, planning, thought analysis, risk-reward assessment, will power, urge suppression, moral decisions, and evaluating and benefiting from experience.

When you get into a flow state naturally because you're only motivation is being completely involved in the activity for its own sake, the brain turns off some of its features, including the prefrontal cortex, literally freeing mental bandwidth so you get laser focus. This is called transient or temporary hypo-frontality.

Ego is not active and you begin to merge your awareness of the action with the action itself. You lose all self-consciousness and personal reflection. You don't self-monitor as you go along because your logical linear mind is turned off. You don't try to think yourself through the next move. You effortlessly choose in each moment and make adjustments and course corrections simultaneously as you work. You're in the zone.

How Do You Hack a Flow State?

Flow is a state of super awareness and all characteristics of being there happen simultaneously.

- Concentration - intense and focused on the present moment.

- Personal control over the activity - everything seems to be happening through you rather than because of you.

- Time distortion - you lose track of time because your sense of self fades and you have hyper-focused awareness.

- Motivation - an experience of the task at hand being intrinsically rewarding; if there's no sense of meaning, there will be no motivation.

- Challenge and skill must be equal - the highest level of flow is achieved when it's matched with a high skill level.

If you want to experience flow more often you must be curious and persistent with a passion for the activity or subject. You must prefer challenges that stimulate and motivate you. The intensity of the situation you willingly put yourself into can put you into flow.

But passion and drive are not enough to bring about high-intensity flow.

- Learn the ropes or fundamentals of a skill.

- Stretch beyond your comfort zone but don't make it too difficult.

- Learn in stages.

A musician who gets on stage and fluidly improvises has practiced many years. He doesn't have to think about where the keys or strings are. He can simultaneously play the instrument and create the sound he wants without analyzing it. There is no thinking process involved. He's in flow. You must prepare until the fundamentals are second nature.

Flow states are not limited to artistic endeavors. You can reach flow doing math or problem solving, running, in competition, doing housework or working on an assembly line. As long as you're motivated and see the intrinsic value in an effort, you can reach flow.

Getting into the Zone

A good way to get into flow is through meditation. During meditation you create new neural pathways and open up more brain neurons to being more focused. Practicing meditation will teach you how to get into flow state but it can take many years of persistence to master. Most people can't stick with it long enough to get to the level they want to achieve.

Brain wave technology has been used by more than 2 million people in 193 countries and has been researched and studied at Mt. Sinai Medical Center in New York. Brainwave entrainment, you get all the benefits and brain wave patterns of lifelong meditational practice without the learning curve, without the struggle, in about 1/8 the time.

Your passions serve an essential purpose. They keep you balanced and energized and give you optimism and a rich inner life. Your brain is the only thing that can put you into a state of flow. You may fail several times, but at some point, you'll come out of flow only to realize that you've actually been there.

Visualizing Your Life

The reason you struggle to carry efforts or ideas to completion is because you're trying to live out a resolution using the tools previously acquired by and stored within—imprinted on—your brain. This is the reason you struggle, but it will eventually be the reason you succeed.

What does that mean? Aren't they the same thing? You've resolved to do something so you must intend to do it, right?

Much of what we see is simply the product of someone's imagination, of how some individuals viewed the world and of what they thought the world needed. They were powerful, persuasive and capable of making the civilized world "happen", working it to their benefit or in the case of an altruistic endeavor, to the benefit of the community at large. They envisioned a world or some part of it the way they wanted it to be. They saw it, they felt it, they lived and breathed it in their minds and they made it happen.

How about if you begin to imagine, envision yourself, you being that person doing or being what you want to be? If you'll do that enough, your subconscious mind will believe it. The subconscious mind does not know the difference. It sees life in movies. It doesn't know what's real. That's why you're terrified when you go get in your car after a scary movie in a theater. Your subconscious mind is telling you to be afraid. It's still watching the movie.

The God-given Laws which govern consciousness do not waver, but understanding the techniques you can use and stick with will make the difference. The Laws are working whether you're aware of them or not. As an example, when Bill Gates gives away money, he's going to give it away whether you're aware of it or not, but it would certainly be better for you if you knew when, where, and how to be a part of that gifting.

So how do you practically use your imagination to change your world view (perspective)?

The answer is meditation and visualization.

Meditation can take years to master, and visualization can easily turn to random chaos without the benefit of focus. Our lives are busy and often unorganized, messy, and complicated, so we find little time to do anything that's actually peaceful. We're constantly distracted by media, social media, technology, household tasks, and family obligations. If you find yourself having difficulty with either of these (meditation or visualization), both can be easily learned and are not difficult to master with the help of binaural beats. In Appendices II and III, you'll discover just how easy this can be.

This is where you'll use the power of your imagination to get the inspiration you need to make your dreams for your life become a reality.

Imagineering: The Practical Side of Imagining

In 1990, the word imagineering was trademarked by Disney Enterprises, Inc., but the word was invented by Alcoa in 1940. A combination of "imagination" and "engineering", it means "implementing creative ideas in practical form" and was applied to such things as urban design, among other things. A Time magazine ad from February 16, 1942, titled "The Place They Do Imagineering" relates the origin of the word:

"For a long time we've sought a word to describe what we all work at hard here at Alcoa... IMAGINEERING is the word... Imagineering is letting your imagination soar, and then engineering it down to earth."[25]

This is what Michael Phelps did when he visualized his race, minute by minute, stroke by stroke, until he got to the finish line in his mind. He imagined himself winning and saw how that would take place every step of the way. He engineered the win in his mind before he made it a reality.

Former professional basketball player, Michael "MJ" Jordan, played several positions throughout his fifteen seasons with the Chicago Bulls, and he excelled at each of them, winning six NBA championships. Before every game, he would play the full game in his mind before going to sleep.

Like Phelps, he used his five senses and their submodalities.

He saw the court, the gleam of the wood, the colors of the other team, the people in the stands, the Spalding logo on the ball; he smelled the sweat, the popcorn, and the fine grain leather; he heard the hollow thump of ball on wood, the swoosh as it passed through the hoop, the squeak of rubber on the court, and the race of thundering feet as they moved around him. He felt the ball securely in his hand and his middle finger touching the seam before a free throw.

Both Phelps and Jordan dreamed it and made it real for them. But these are experiences that these men have had repeatedly. They knew what to expect; they knew how their chosen game was played.

But what if you don't have a set career or something you've been doing a long time and just want to get better at? What should you do? What should you visualize?

You can picture a blank canvas or chalkboard and fill it with anything you want to be, do or have. This is all part of the visualization technique that's so effective in allowing you to manifest your desires through your imagination. And you can do this in your mind or a Mind Map on a real blank board, called a visualization board, or both.

Create your Mind Map with clip images or photos, and use any material you want that represents what you want. Don't just put up a picture of any house, for example. Find one that comes as close as possible to the house of your dreams.

You can take this a step further by seeing yourself in a big screen movie in your mind, complete with sound. Watch yourself go through the motions of unlocking the front door to your new house, driving that car you've always wanted. Maybe it's a convertible. Is your hair blowing in the wind? Is the radio on? Is anyone with you? The more details you provide, the more real you will be able to "see" this happening for you. (See Appendix III: Guided Visualization)

Designing Your Mission Statement

Along with visualizing what you want, you will create affirmations (your vision statement Vision Map). This is a Mind Map. These are the things that affirm what you want and which you will repeat often, every day. They'll be what keeps you motivated. Seeing them hung on your refrigerator or bathroom wall will keep you focused on moving in the direction of your dreams; they'll remind you that everything you do now must be in alignment with getting you to your desires.

You can recite your affirmations at any time, but they're particularly affective just before you go into meditation or a binaural beats session. The idea is not to set a deadline or particular goal, but to envision the direction you must take to fine tune your actions. Your affirmations must be something you believe, not just some random phony goal just to see if it works.

You can also use modeling; a means of visualizing yourself as being like or as successful as someone else. This goes back to Joe Stumpf's work with Ultimate Scenarios. Find and observe someone you admire or strive to be like and model how they've achieved results. Don't be afraid to ask questions, even if you don't know this person personally. Research them, see if you can somehow meet with them. Be honest and authentic and you might be surprised how responsive people can be to helping someone else, particularly if it doesn't cost them anything but a little time.

I talk a bit more about affirmations in Appendix III: Visualization

Science: Using Mental Power to Create Epigenetic Change

Ironically, modern technology is using the model of a self-healing wound to create self-healing software that allows complex computerized applications to recover from faults and regain normative performance.[26]

For some people, this is the perfect analogy. They may be more likely to believe they can transform their thoughts and beliefs if they see that a computer can do it, and that the design was based on the way biological systems heal themselves. We now have self-healing armor, self-healing fabric, self-healing electronic circuitry and self-healing plastics among other things. These items can literally "detect" when they're scratched, torn or broken and initiate "healing" or repair of the compromised component. There's actually a self-healing polymer that "fixes" itself under ultraviolet light, and many of these inventions were developed based on the way human cells work, the way blood clots or the way skin heals.

Should humans be capable of doing any less than these inanimate objects?

Although the ancient art of self-healing has been mastered by many people, most of them are involved in Traditional Chinese or Eastern Medicine, yoga, qi gong, tai chi, acupuncture, and other-than-mainstream lifestyle methods. Most of the successful healers in the world are no smarter than you are. Their intelligence and common sense may not be keener nor is their knowledge obtained from books and education greater.

What they do possess is the right kind of experience and knowledge of how the Universe works. Specifically, what stands between you and your future successes is what you believe to be true about yourself and the world in which you live. We all "become" the laws and notions we believe in.

Epigenetics is the study of modifying gene expression. Instead of altering the genetic code itself to change the outcome or behavior of a cell, the way a gene behaves is modified using external sources through DNA, which is responsible for turning genes on or off as necessary. The DNA sequence is not changed, only the way in which it instructs cells.

To make this simple, DNA is to cells what the brain is to the body. Our brain tells us what to do, whether it's a laugh response, muscle action such as lifting or grasping, or breathing. It doesn't tell the body to grow only one arm or leg (unless there's some mutation of genes). In the same sense, DNA sets the function of genes and instructs them on what to do or how they should express.

Today, the ground-breaking study of the modification of gene expression, known as epigenetics, tells us that our environment and external factors can have an influence on what we become and also that we have the capacity to change that.

The animal kingdom is a good way to demonstrate the power of genes, and by default the power of the mind. In some species, animals that are born during winter have thicker coats than their siblings who might be born in the summer.

Each generation passes on the encoded and external information that affects their physical condition in an intricate and multifaceted interface between genes, the environment, and internal intent.

What if we, as individuals, could learn to copy these epigenetic processes and control our own cells? What if we could tell them how to behave by thinking in the correct way or speaking the right words?

The information we need to successfully transform our lives is already deep within us, within our memory. It will require dedication, patience, and persistence. Your environment must be filled with optimism and focused intention. This is where you will begin the entire mental process of the Can You DIGG It? system.

In Effect of Conscious Intention on Human DNA,[27] Dr. Glen Rein, Ph.D. and Director at the Quantum Biology Research Lab in Northport, NY, talks about the effects of focused intention.

"The effect of focused intention is often referred to as psychokinesis, and mind-body medicine has well recognized the ability of mental images, generated by the mind and directed to specific parts of the body, to produce profound physiological changes. Healing research has demonstrated that various types of healers can produce biological effects, and a third line of investigation involves the study of Chi-Gong practitioners who can also influence biological systems.

"A study on goal-directed healing of a tumor was conducted using five different mental intentions and different contents of consciousness by a professional healer. Five methods were used and two emerged as having sufficient biological activity and cohering of energy resulting in observable change in the tumor.

1. The intention for returning to the natural order and harmony of the cell's normal rate of growth

2. The intention for letting God's will flow through his hands

3. Unconditional love with no specific direction to the energy being given

"The first method, with a specific intent of returning the natural harmony of the cell, was 39% effective in inhibiting the tumor's growth, with the second being only half as effective. Sending unconditional love with no specific intention had no effect.

The study showed that, by changing the thought and image content of a given state of consciousness, it's possible to observe different biological effects, and that non-focused thought has no effect.

"The results are remarkable since not only could a different biological response be observed by changing the mental image, but an actual reversal of the biological process of cell growth was achieved. By concentrating on returning the cells to their natural order, while holding no visual image, intention could be separated from imagery. This experiment demonstrated that intention produced the same 20% inhibitory effect as did imagery alone. On the other hand, when the image of few cells in the petri dish was combined with the intention for the cells to return to their natural order, the inhibitory effect on cell growth was doubled to 40%. These results therefore suggest that imagery and intent each contributed equally to inhibiting the growth of tumor cells in culture and that their effect is additive when combined together."

There may be no ultimate state to which we can aspire. Think about that! We may hold somewhere within us unlimited powers of perception, love, creation and more! We can create new realities using our imagination, with endless possibilities for painting our personal canvas. When we live through our imagination, nothing is impossible. Problems are solvable; space and time become irrelevant, and we can choose to live in a world of our own making.

The path we choose to take may be long or short, but if you focus on it with open mind, you will find all the answers to questions that have limited the power and potential of your imagination.

I'd like to share with you a little story that perfectly exemplifies the power you have within you:

> A young boy sat listening to a story being told by his grandfather.

"There are two wolves within you that are fighting all the time. They will tear at each other until the one is defeated and the other prevails."

"But how will I know which one will prevail?" asked the boy.

"It will be the one that you feed," replied the old man. (Unknown)

There is power that goes beyond learning to control your will, your thoughts and your mind. There are miracles that can occur beyond the laws of physics. In fact, when it comes to consciousness, there are no rules, at least as far as man can presently detect. If there were, we'd have limits to our imagination, something we currently view as limitless and without bounds.

"Luke Skywalker: "I do not believe it."

Yoda: "That is why you will fail."

The more you can connect with the source of all energy, the more energy you're going to receive. This is the beginning of the progression toward powerful transformation.

I have found several books to be highly inspirational for me for several reasons. They had a profound impact on my life and I'd like to share them with you.

1. *The Secret* by Rhonda Byrne

This book is about the Law of Attraction. It contains wisdom from modern-day teachers who have used the great "secret to life" to achieve health, wealth, and happiness. You'll hear from great teachers, thinkers, and influencers such as philosopher Bob Proctor, metaphysician Dr. Joe Vitale, entrepreneur John Assaraf, personal transformation specialist Dr. John DeMartini, psychologist Dr. Denis Waitley, visionary Michel Beckwith, motivational speaker Jack Canfield, thought leader Wallace Wattles, and author and metaphysical speaker Neville Goddard.

It contains their incredible inspiring stories of acquiring massive wealth, overcoming disease, and achieving what many would regard as impossible. And it runs the gamut of various explanations and interpretations of how the Law of Attraction works.

"We all work with one Infinite Power. We all guide ourselves by exactly the same laws. The natural laws of the universe are so precise... that everything that's coming into your life you are attracting. And it's attracted to you by virtue of the images you're holding in your mind." (Bob Proctor)

One of my personal favorite speakers from The Secret is Neville Goddard, one of the pioneers of the modern-day philosophy behind the Law of Attraction. In "Neville Goddard's Method for Creating Reality", Maxwell Akin writes:

"Imagination is a tool that can conjure anything. Images. Smells. Tastes. Sounds. Sights. Anything at all. But without the feelings that come from such a thing, reality remains somewhat unchanged. You see, Neville Goddard knew that you can imagine that which you desire as much as you like, and there is tremendous value in doing just that, make no mistake. But without the feelings that come from the fulfillment of your desire, then there is nothing, for feelings are a language in and of themselves, and if you know how to speak the language of God, if you know how to speak directly to that infinite faculty within yourself, then there is nothing that can or will stop you."[28]

"It is not what you want that you attract, you attract what you believe to be true."

— Neville Goddard

If you haven't read this book or seen the full length video, I hope you'll take the time to do so. It will blow your mind and certainly give you food for thought!

2. *The Science of Getting Rich* by Wallace Wattles

"A man develops in mind, soul, and body by making use of things, and society is so organized that man must have money in order to become the possessor of things, therefore, the basis of all advancement for man must be the science of getting rich." (Wallace Wattles, The Science of Getting Rich)

What is it about money that people lie, steal, and even kill for it? Money is not the root of evil, but the love of money might be. In this book, Wattles explains how to transform your approach to money from a Christian perspective. In fact, The Science of Getting Rich was the inspiration behind Rhonda Byrne's The Secret.

I learned to think creatively rather than competitively, and how this is one of the keys to becoming wealthy. I was able to move forward and set myself on the right course for obtaining wealth in an ethical way. And I was able to succeed at doing what I want to do. And it's all done through the philosophy behind the Law of Attraction, learning exactly how to control thoughts and emotions, and make the right decisions to achieve the success we were created for.

I also learned that it's not enough just to wish for something or want something, but that it's important to be specific and detailed in what I want. This was the inspiration for my book I AM. I had a longing to be what I wanted to be, but my images were vague and uninformed. I was inspired to overcome any mental laziness, which I didn't even realize I had at the time, and change my thinking as well as the power and strength of my intentions for my life.

3. *Think and Grow Rich* **by Napoleon Hill**

This is one of the oldest books on the subject, and was originally published during the Great Depression, but it's sold over 100 million copies. It's all about personal development and the philosophy of achievement presented as 13 principles drawn from the success stories of greats as Andrew Carnegie, Henry Ford and other millionaires of his time.

He talks about suppressing negative thoughts and keeping your focus on the long term using Desire, Imagination, Planning, Decision, and Persistence among other things. He also agrees that the subconscious mind is the powerhouse behind what we believe, what we think, and what we manifest.

Hill believed "The object of all life is development; and everything that lives has an inalienable right to all the development it is capable of attaining. Man's right to life means his right to have the free and unrestricted use of all the things which may be necessary to his fullest mental, spiritual, and physical unfoldment; or, in other words, his right to be rich.

Can You DIGG It? I knew that you could!

7.

THE FIFTH POWER: G: THE POWER OF GOING WITH ACTION

"The path to success is to take massive determined action."

- Anthony Robbins

All of this is going to take some work. If it didn't, everyone would be successful. But the fact that is requires massive action should not deter you from reaching for what you want.

Take a good look at your life and current living conditions. If you don't like structure and routine, you're easily overwhelmed, you keep making excuses as to why you can't change or get things done, you have a serious lack of time management skills, or you keep avoiding responsibilities, it's very likely you have become a procrastinator.

Your level of determination is likely to fade even before you finish reading this book. Like most people, you may not be willing to go the extra mile. But the fact that you're reading this book and got this far into it means you have something within you that's driving you to go further, maybe further than others are willing to go. I promise you, if you are willing to get through this chapter, you will begin to understand that you don't have to live like this anymore. You don't have to spend your life wishing you could just get off the couch and start making your dreams come true. BE more, DO more, and HAVE more. It only takes one positive change to trigger a cascade.

Staying Motivated

I've found when we Imagine correctly enough times, taking action is easy. There's no fear because we've already experience what's going to happen in our imagination. So if you have trouble "Going", then revisit the last chapter.

And that's true for all chapters, if you have a challenge with one, then reread the previous one. If you can't imagine something for yourself, then you should revisit your decided desires. If you have trouble deciding your desires, then you should reread The Power of Identity.

If you have trouble with knowing who you are, your Identity, then reread the Power of Beliefs.

So maybe you're passionate about what you want. You've learned to visualize it and you've set a concrete plan for getting there. But let's face it, we're all human and subject to moments of self-doubt. When you find yourself losing steam, there are some practical ways to rejuvenate your engine.

Make a Mind Map. These maps used to be called creativity boards and have been used by some of the most successful people in the world. Put words, images, questions, or anything else that will give you inspiration onto a board or a MindMap template. (You can get one free by contacting me at johndiggs.com or go to MindMeister.com and use code DIGGIT for a discount) The idea behind this is to have a clear image of who you want to become or what you want to create. Once your pattern emerges, you're on to your passion. Your maps may begin to look like a family tree with many branches or a river with many tributaries. This is exactly what you want.

Map all your achievements. Why should you do this? Because it will help you to design yourself. Look at your Map and acknowledge the effort and commitment it took to achieve them. Keeping track of your successes will give you encouragement whenever you need it. Don't discount the small stuff, like getting an A on a test or showing up on time every day for practice.

Discover your strong points. What holds many people back is their inability to see the opportunities for their particular talent or skills. Have someone you trust take a look at your Map with a fresh eye and write the potential opportunities you may not see.

Get moving. Map out all the things you would do if you had the proper resources and enough money. Map things you would do for free because you love doing them and things you would do if you never had to work another day in your life. Compare this to your Map of all your talents and skills. Look at all your Maps. Some things may be repetitive. Try to find some common denominator. This will lead you to unlocking your potential.

Follow through. Following through is another key to making this work. You can't say you want something then sit at home waiting for opportunity to knock. It's not enough to know what your skills and talents are. You must start to work on them. If you are talented and you don't use, practice, and hone that talent, you won't be any closer to becoming the person you want to be than you are today. You need to practice as often as possible. Doing research is a strong component to developing a skill or talent, too. Find out what's new in that industry and do your best to grow in that direction. By extension, you're going to make a big difference in every area of your life.

Our parents probably wanted something for us, something perhaps they wanted for themselves but never achieved. They would have loved to live vicariously through you, but you must remove all thoughts of what other people want for you. The people closest to your – your family and close friends – will have good insight into what your strong talents are and if you trust them, listen to their input, but don't listen to anyone who tells you that you can't do something.

If you've managed to hone in on that one thing you think is right for you but you're not willing to devote as much time and energy to it as possible, it's not the right path for you. Please revisit the Power of Decision.

Don't think about how you're going to do something, just begin. If it's something you love and it's right for you, it will not seem like work.

When I talk about putting all your energy into this one thing, don't do what I did. Don't stress over it so much that you make yourself sick. Nothing is worth that. Use what available time you have and don't spread yourself too thin. If you do, everything you attempt will suffer. If you're hungry for it, if your heart is in it, you will succeed. Decide what you want, set your intention, stay positive, and put some time into it.

What Does it Mean to Take Massive Action?

Simply put, it means thinking of your goal as an obligation and a responsibility. You must own this including the problems, obstacles, mistakes, and failures that are going to go with it. This is going to be an on-going evolutionary process, so be prepared to put yourself out there.

- Apply ever-increasing amounts of energy to the thing you want to accomplish.

- Increase your level of effort in order to build momentum.

- Expect more from yourself by raising your personal standards of productivity or action.

- Set the bar for tasks higher and keep them in alignment with your vision.

- Take steps to expand your knowledge base. The more you do the more you'll learn. The more you learn, the more you'll be able to do.

- Take advantage of opportunities as they present themselves. Don't be lazy. Every opportunity has the potential to bring you more opportunities.

But just because you think big and have grand visions for your life, doesn't mean it's going to happen. You must follow through by taking massive action to bring your vision to reality.

Achievement coach and mind mapper Adam Sicinski[29] offers this advice on how to break mental barriers and take massive action:

1. Clarify your desire. Make it specific and concrete, not vague.

2. Get ready to get out of your comfort zone and make peace with what's to come. There will be setbacks, unknowns, obstacles, and failures.

3. Understand that you can't know everything, and get rid of your fear of uncertainty.

4. Commit, commit, commit.

5. Stay motivated either by thinking about how great things are going to be if you follow through or by thinking about how bad things will be if you don't follow through. This is your leverage on yourself to keep going.

6. Expect to have to make some sacrifices. This just comes with the territory.

7. Act as though you have a deadline. This will give you a sense of urgency. Stop saying "mañana". If you're passionate about achieving whatever it is you want for yourself, this will give you the drive and urgency you need.

8. Don't be afraid to take some risks. Just do whatever it takes to get the job done. Learn to look forward to the challenges that are coming and also the rewards they will bring.

9. Always be thinking about the next step. No excuses.

10. Think unreasonably, outside the box.

To think unreasonably means to think about what's possible; about what could be done; about what could be achieved if you took a specific kind of action. Where other people think narrowly about what needs to happen, you instead have a broad perspective that takes many possibilities into consideration."

-Adam Sicinski

Goal Setting: Where Do You Want to Be?

Don't worry too much in the beginning about exactly how you're going to achieve your goals or get to your desired dream. Just concern yourself with taking the proper steps and doors will open for you, showing you people, resources, ideas, and everything else you need but were unable to 'see' before.

"Going" or taking action means you have faith that you will experience your desires at the perfect and right moment. Until then, continue to imagine yourself succeeding while taking massive action steps towards your goals, with the faith that it will happen according to the God-given laws of the Universe. If you don't apply faith and believe that this is possible for you, your dream will remain a fantasy.

In Chapter 5: The Power of Decision, you began to understand how important making decisions is. Start today to define an accurate description of what you want to do, even something as simple as signing up for a newsletter or joining a club that aligns with your goals. Knowing what you want to achieve and believing you can achieve it are the first steps to getting there.

1. **Think it.** Everything begins in your heart and mind. Every achievement, great or small, began in someone's thoughts and came from their desires. So what if you dream of something big? What if you were allowed to have anything, regardless of time, money or resources? What would that be? You want to be a dreamer of all the possibilities for yourself, your family and your business.

2. **Believe it.** You can dream big, but your dream for yourself must be believable. You must be able to believe that if certain things take place, if certain criteria are met, it can be accomplished. Here's an example: A person with no college education can dream of building a $20 million-a-year

business. This is a big deal but it's entirely believable if this person takes the right steps. A ninety year old woman with crippling arthritis in her hips, knees and ankles who hasn't exercised in twenty-five years will run a 20k in under two hours. It's big, but not very likely and therefore not believable. She stands a better chance of building a $20 million a year company.

3. **Visualize it.** I've talked a lot about the Power of Imagination. A great achiever has the ability to 'see' his desired end result in his mind's eye. He pictures himself right in the thick of whatever it is he wants – sitting at his desk as the CEO of his new corporate headquarters even if he's sitting on a plastic garden chair in his garage 'headquarters'. What you 'rehearse' in your mind is the imprint your subconscious will believe is real. Remember, the subconscious doesn't know the difference between what actually happened and what you tell it has happened over and over again. (Learn more about how to visualize in Appendix III: Guided Visualization.) So what pictures are you playing in your mind?

4. **Share it.** This is a big one. Many people like to keep their visions and dreams a secret. They believe that telling others about their plans will put a jinx on them or that someone will steal their ideas. Nothing could be farther from the truth. Unless you have a patentable idea without a patent, don't keep it all to yourself. Don't leave it a quiet dream that has no energy. The more you 'say' it, in this case by telling others about it, the more energy you give to it. The more often you tell others about your plans, the more you will start to believe it yourself. Keep in mind that when I refer

to believing it, I'm referring to your subconscious mind, so always think in those terms.

5. **Plan it.** A dream without a plan is just a fantasy. Things rarely 'just happen'. Most things that 'just happened' were the product of much planning and preparation and thought. Honing your plans is something you'll need to do on a regular basis, thinking through details, writing them down and breaking them into manageable tasks. Set a timeframe for achieving each portion of your plan, but don't be discouraged if you hit a snag and miss your deadline. Adjust your plan, find any flaws and recalculate your timeframe. Keep moving. I encourage you to use my mind mapping tools. Join me in a free webinar at johndiggs.com

6. **Research it.** As you start out to accomplish each task in your plan, your Mind Map, you will inevitably be doing research, seeking out books, classes, tutorials, and mentors along the way. Take time to allow others into this. You will discover that information can come from the most unlikely places. Even the most seemingly insignificant conversation can lead you to a gem of knowledge that can help you reach your goals. Don't discount what others have to offer to your game plan. That doesn't mean you should follow someone else's council, with the possible exception of a mentor or expert in the field, but you are the one who will make any final decisions regarding how to proceed.

7. **Work on it.** We would all like to sit at the beach and let the world come to us on a silver platter. But successful people are generally the hardest workers, not surprisingly. Successful people consistently work on their goals. If you work every day, even in small degrees, on what you want to achieve, you will get there in the end. At some point, you

will pick up steam and your work will have what's known as a 'snowball effect'. The more you see happen in the right direction, the more you will want to put energy into achieving your goals. Keep your vision up front in your mind and push yourself. You are that CEO. You have that full membership. You have lost all that weight.

8. **Enjoy it.** Don't forget to balance your life with the joy of living. Enjoy the process of planning, working toward and building your vision into reality. Yes, it will be work but knowing where it will lead is what will keep you going. You will need to apply self-discipline, lots of it. A good strategy is to reward yourself along the way, perhaps at certain milestones in your plan. This could take the form of treating yourself to dinner at a luxury restaurant, taking the weekend to go camping or doing something else you enjoy. You might even consider a weekend seminar to be a reward and something you want to do, and if it pertains to your goal, you're killing two birds with one stone!

"All men dream, but not equally. Those who dream by night in the dusty recesses of their minds wake in the day to find that all was vanity [in vain]. But the dreamers of the day are dangerous men, for they may act their dream with open eyes and make it possible."

- T. E. Lawrence

You must be determined in your efforts, reinforcing your belief that what you want to achieve is possible. You must take the responsibility for your actions or inactions. You must educate yourself regarding the steps you need to take to get to where you want to be, reorganizing or adjusting your plan along the way as more doors and opportunities open for you. You must be motivated to take action. This is the only way to get to where you want to be.

> *"The future belongs to those who believe in the beauty of their dreams."*
>
> – Eleanor Roosevelt

Setting goals with deadlines creates a tangible expectation, something your mind can relate to and something it can convert into physical reality. If you want to achieve anything, you must master goal-setting. Don't overwhelm yourself with pressures that will only result in harmful stress. You can take it slowly, but you must set goals with deadlines for completion of tasks within that plan. (I talk more about how to determine what you want from life in my book I AM).

- **See it, say it, and Map it.** Many of us were taught in school to "see it (read it), say it out loud, and write it down". This is the step that reinforces what you've put into your subconscious. Setting a goal and mapping it is a physical reminder of exactly what needs to be done.

- **Break it down.** Spend time and energy on the tasks you've broken down in your Map, chipping away at them daily, readjusting when something goes wrong and continuing to move in the direction of that goal or plan. Breaking it down into manageable tasks allows you to see the order in which things need to be done.

- **Set timelines.** This will give you a clear picture of when you need to accomplish this portion of the plan. Setting a timeline for each task within your plan will keep you on track so you don't become overwhelmed. Be honest with yourself about how much time you have available to do these things. You may already have a fulltime job, a family and home to take care of or any number of other commitments. Understand what you need to do and be practical about it.

There are many time management training tools available but for me, the most useful is the S.M.A.R.T. method which first appeared in the November 1981 issue of Management Review. It perfectly explains how goals should be set up. I encourage you to move forward by joining my **SMART Method Mind Map Free Webinar** at www.johndiggs.com/mindmaps.

The S.M.A.R.T. Method

(S) – Specific. A goal should be clearly defined, using details to describe specifically what the goal will be. So it's not enough to say "I want to lose weight." You must specify exactly what amount you want to lose. "I want to lose twenty pounds."

(M) – Measurable. You must be able to measure a clear beginning and ending to your goal, with measurable results. "I want to lose twenty pounds in thirty days."

(A) – Active. You must take all the responsibility for achieving the goal. "I'm going to lose twenty pounds if I ever get enough time to go to the gym" is a passive statement that puts no responsibility on you. Instead, say "I'm going to lose twenty pounds by the end of January."

(R) – Realistic. Once again, any goal you set for yourself must be realistic. "I'm going to lose one hundred pounds in thirty days" is not only unrealistic, it's dangerous, but losing twenty pounds in thirty days is very realistic and doable with the proper tools and actions.

(T) – Time Bound. Every goal must have a timeframe within which it will be completed. Businesses don't reach goals by saying to their employees "Here's a project for you, but it really doesn't matter when you get it done." This goes back to building deadlines into your plan. When will you have those twenty pounds off, exactly?

Each of these steps is critical to accomplishing the tasks you've built into your plan and they will keep you organized regarding where you are in the process. Having your S.M.A.R.T. plan in place on a Mind Map will allow you to focus on getting there, rather than trying to remember what you have to do and when.

Please visit johndiggs.com/mindmaps to see and request a copy of the S.M.A.R.T Goals Mind Map, which I created for you to reference and use as a template.

Recording Your Victories

I've talked a little bit about recording your victories, achievement, awards, and honors. You've touched on this in one of the Maps you made to help you hone in on your identity, your authentic self.

It's not uncommon for people who think negatively to forget about all the little successes they've had along the way. They behave as though the small things don't matter, don't amount to or mean anything. Instead they focus on what they consider all the failures in their lives.

Most of us need a little help in discovering our talents. We need validation. But you don't need to rely on the kindness of strangers to validate your life. Start keeping a Success Map.

On this Mind Map, you'll simply put down all the successes you've had, however large or small. Each consecutive success will branch out from a previous one if there is a connection. For example, if you were assigned a special project at work and the boss gave you kudos, this is a recordable success. If you and your brainstorming team later went out for a bite to eat and you discovered you had more in common with someone on the team than either of you suspected, making this new friend is a branch of that success. When you get a raise because that project success counted in your favor, this is also a branch of that success.

Everything counts. If you're a parent with a disciplining problem, each time you effectively make your child stick to the boundaries you've set up, this is a success. When that child finally sticks to these boundaries on his or her own, this is a branch of that success. You get the idea.

Making this Mind Map will encourage you and help you grow. This is a bit different than keeping a diary. What you'll do is write down, every day or night, any small successes you had during that day, such as sticking to your diet, gaining a new opportunity, completing a task on your goal plan, finishing a book, stepping out of your comfort zone in any way; anything that is positive is a success.

This is part of self-love. When you're feeling low, like you're not getting anywhere, go through your Mind Maps and read all the successes you've had. Ask yourself why you succeeded at them. What did you do differently? Why did you work? How do you feel about completing this? While you're asking yourself these questions, remember that you are the one who accomplished this. This simple strategy will go a long way to encouraging you and keeping you on track.

We all tend to remember the big highlights that take place in our lives, but it's all the small-scale successes that add up to great self-esteem.

Can You DIGG It? I knew that you could!

8.

THE SIXTH POWER:
G: THE POWER OF GUIDING
YOUR GIFT

The human mind is a complex machine. It has the capacity to generate, analyze and process an average of 1000 thoughts per second, all of which get channeled through neuro-pathways. This is a skill which we don't have to learn; it's part of how we're naturally wired.

But how you craft those thoughts and how your subconscious mind interprets them is largely instructed by all the external inputs throughout your life: childhood, culture, training or groups, indoctrination, physical environment, and your natural tendencies or disposition.

The human mind is always in the process of leaning either toward being protective (Negative Mind) or projective (Positive Mind). The mediator, the Neutral Meditative Mind, will weigh the value—the pluses and minuses—given by the Negative and Positive, and your decisions will be made based on the weight it places on each.

We protect ourselves from danger by first calculating any risk/ threat, then we determine the positive aspects of an effort or enterprise, at which point we move to the Meditative Neutral where we balance the two.

Each aspect of our generated thoughts and how we interpret those thoughts informs how we interact with our surroundings, people and daily life. And there are several challenges.

- The first challenge is to balance the head and the heart in humility, creativity, and beauty.

- Listen to the Negative and the Positive. The Negative does not imply a negative connotation; it's simply the opposite of the Positive. Its function is protective; it strengthens discipline and crafts integrity. It gives us the gifts of containment and discernment. The challenge here is to avoid becoming pessimistic.

- On the other hand, the Positive Mind is expansive. It inspires us by telling us what the possible gain is in a situation, but this can lead to idealism in the extreme, where we ignore any danger or potential loss.

- The Neutral Mind listens to both the Negative and Positive and leads us to the best decision. The challenge here is a tendency toward indecision or difficulty perceiving the larger picture.

As you proceed through learning to balance your thoughts and guide them, and as you grow in this area, you'll get to the point where you are now guiding your life on a grand scale. You'll be better able to focus and manifest projected thoughts and desires.

Abstract concepts of thought will begin to become concrete and practical.

Remember, the God-given Law of Attraction is clear and unfailing. We attract into our lives what we think about most. Thoughts are active and billions of them pass through our minds, many of which are the same thoughts repeating themselves over and over again from day to day. But some thoughts are more active than others. These thoughts are the ones that will evoke a response that makes you "feel" something, whether it's a good feeling or a bad feeling.

Most thoughts don't invoke feelings so they don't hold much power, they don't increase or decrease your vibrational frequency and therefore don't attract much of anything. They simply come and go, passing through relatively unnoticed.

A repetitive thought that makes you miserable such as, "I have to get up again and go to work" is really just a passing thought but you've given it some power by repeating it every morning. It's not a thought that is making you happy but you've "activated" it to a power level.

Substitute a thought that has the reverse effect such as, "I'm so thankful that I have a job to go to so I can make money to bring me closer to my goal." This is the way the Law works. It will work regardless of what you think, so why not make it work for you rather than against you?

Everything you put out there or project is what's reflected back to you. This is the Law of Projection.

Willing the God in You: Using God's Energy

We live in a multi-dimensional world, with the ideal life on Earth being lived in the physical, mental and spiritual. To be successful, you need to set up daily priorities that not only keep you on track and are in accordance with your vision, but that create a balance in body, mind and spirit.

You don't necessarily need to spend a lot of time on any one thing, but keep in mind that what you do spend time on and the people you spend it with will impact the direction and outcome of your life.

Going for the next level—drawing on God's energy—involves a focus on those things that will move you forward without compromising your health and your valuable relationships.

Unless, of course, you aspire to be a monk sitting on top of a mountain.

But willing the God in you does not require you to become a monk, live your life alone and isolated, or join a religious group. You only need to believe that God is within you, that the Universal energy that created all things is also in you. Your capacity to discover that spirit is determined by your willingness to connect with it.

"You won't find Grace if you're not willing to go anywhere near it."

-Hugh Laurie

Once you've meditated on this, you can use God's energy to harmonize and transform your body, your mind and your life in any way you desire.

You are the creator. Your energy is God's energy. God is within you. Find the deepest inclination of your heart and you will have tapped into the source of your potential, not only as man but as

God. You will become connected with the earth, the cosmos and your own primordial power. You will be working with bio-energy, vital life force energy, God's energy.

I truly believe this is the way we communicate with our Higher Power, not with words as much as with vivid imaginings; imagining our desires, just as though they were a prayer. Good prayers are inspired imagination.

This is the way Mike Phelps and Mike Jordan and many others were able to become so successful in their chosen field. They imagined vividly with inspiration; they experienced their desire in their imagination. This is the first step to guiding your gift!

What is Emotional Intelligence?

Humans are blessed with both a rational and an emotional mind. And each of those plays an important part in shaping how we make decisions, how we behave, and how we react to all the challenges and varying situations that are thrown at us each and every day.

Just because someone is smart (has a high IQ), has common sense or street smarts, is talented, rich, good-looking, fit, or comes from a particular culture or background, does not mean they'll be successful.

Think about all the people you know or have read or heard about that started out poor, with no resources or connections or with physical handicaps, and who made it big. They may be no smarter than you or me. What they have in common is emotional intelligence: the ability to regulate and control their emotions so they can make smart decisions; their emotions are facilitative and not debilitative.

Your emotions play a part in your work, relationships, sports, school, home life, and just about everything else you do.

Emotional intelligence affects our ability to manage our thoughts and feelings, and gives us the power to make appropriate decisions that work consistently with our end goal.

People have emotions running through them daily. The ability to control our emotions so that we are able to function throughout our daily lives is referred to as our emotional intelligence or emotional literacy, and it's a key to maturing as a rational human being.

Your emotional literacy is not fixed. As you become aware, you learn to manage emotions. And this involves both social awareness and personal awareness.

Emotions have long been framed as the enemy of business, and for good reason. We can't go around bullying employees, yelling at partners, and blowing up during a negotiation. Emotions were considered an enemy to health because they caused stress. We were told to eliminate them or control them. Because of this, we learned to repress or suppress our emotions of feelings. Men and boys are told not to cry. Women are called various derogatory names when they become "emotional".

As a culture, we've become numb to our emotions and feelings. We don't act on them. We're cut off from a very important part of our psyche. If we do allow feelings to overcome us, they are often overwhelming or debilitating. Some people turn to drugs or alcohol in an attempt to 'forget' their misery or create a temporary false feeling of well-being.

Suppressed emotions can lead to bad tempers and flare-ups, or they can lead to depression and worse.

The next trend in emotional well-being was to "express" our emotions. So we became a culture of whiners and complainers, people who were making demands based on their feelings. "I feel left out, therefore I want to be compensated." "I'm insulted, therefore I want to be compensated." "I'm not happy with my life, therefore I want laws to be changed."

The list can become very long, but the bottom line is this: any of these scenarios, when maintained on a consistent basis, makes it's impossible to develop emotional intelligence. And increasing your EI is the only way you're going to be able to find your why, visualize your life, set your goals, and take action steps that move you in the direction of your big picture.

So let's talk some more about how emotions have a powerful impact on what we do.

In Chapter 3: The 1st Power: CAN: The Power of Beliefs, you learned that your world view is created by what you believe to be true based on your experiences. But the greatest impact on your memory was from those experiences that held the most emotion for you. Whether positive or negative, the extent and strength of the emotion attached to an event is what gave it power in your subconscious mind.

If you could have been aware of your thoughts and feelings as they were happening, would they have had a different impact? A problem will only arise if you attach importance to a negative emotion and carry that energy around with you, allowing it to color your perspective in some way that is debilitating.

A positive emotion can contain energy that is just as strong, but it will be energy that will attract more positivity. So you must consistently check in on yourself, making sure you're not allowing negative thoughts and emotions to linger.

I talked about energy manipulation earlier, and this goes for both positive and negative energy. But the more positive your energy, the more you will attract what you want.

Esther Hicks is an inspirational speaker who believes that individuals are physical extensions of the non-physical. This is exactly what I mean when I tell you that we are spiritual beings having a human experience. She teaches that we are creators who use our thoughts and intentions to create, which is what I'm teaching you here. The nature of Spirit and the Universe is life-affirming. Once you understand how emotions are part of the human realm, you'll get the idea that you can control them. It's as easy as changing your mind.

The Abraham-Hicks Emotional Guidance Scale represents a hierarchy of emotions that range from fear and desperation at the bottom, the lowest energy, to joy, love, and appreciation at the top, the highest energy.

Here's the emotional scale[30] as described by Abraham-Hicks:

- Joy/Appreciation/Empowerment/Freedom/Love
- Passion
- Enthusiasm/Eagerness/Happiness
- Positive Expectation/Belief
- Optimism
- Hopefulness
- Contentment
- Boredom
- Pessimism
- Frustration/Irritation/Impatience
- Feeling Overwhelmed
- Disappointment
- Doubt
- Worry

- Blame

- Discouragement

- Anger

- Revenge

- Hatred/Rage

- Jealousy

- Insecurity/Guilt/Unworthiness

- Fear/Grief/Desperation/Despair/Powerlessness

Please visit johndiggs.com/mindmaps to access the **Emotional Scale Mind Map** I created for you to determine what emotions you feel most and what feelings you would like to feel more and less of.

Recognize these emotions. When you take stock of how you're feeling, you will find yourself somewhere on this scale. You can certainly improve your thoughts and move up the scale, but you can also backslide. That's why it's important to be consciously aware of what you're thinking and feeling. The idea is to always be striving to reach the ultimate emotion of love, the universal energy.

Four Skills to Increase Emotional Intelligence

Below, I've laid out the 4 skills you will need to develop in order to increase your EI. Remember, mastering your emotions, learning to keep them regulated instead of out of control, will help you make the right decisions to keep you on track to your goal of having, doing, and being what you desire.

1. **Self-awareness.** The first step is to get these feelings out of your head.

- **The problem:** You consistently find yourself sad, angry, jealous, or frustrated. Write down the things that make you feel this way. It doesn't matter what they are. Just get them out of your head.

- **The solution:** Begin to become aware of each time you feel this way. You'll quickly notice a pattern of what triggers these feelings.

- **The goal:** To recognize your own emotions and how they affect your thoughts and behavior.

2. **Social awareness.** Think about others' feelings.

   - **The problem:** You really don't care about how you hurt others. You're not interested in anyone else, even your friends and family, on a deeper level.

   - **The solution:** Learn to listen. Everyone has needs, not just you. Learn to have empathy and put yourself in someone else's shoes.

   - **The goal:** To be able to pick up on emotional cues and recognize the power dynamics within in a group.

3. **Self-management.** Control your emotional impulses.

   - **The problem:** You get depressed easily; you blow up when you can't get your way or when something goes wrong. You make decisions when you're upset.

   - **The solution:** Every time you lose control of your emotions, when you calm down, write it down or map it. Keep track. Again, you'll notice a pattern. Although you may not be able to do anything about it in the moment, eventually you'll begin to lessen how often you lose control.

- **The goal:** To be able to control impulsive behaviors that debilitate you and alienate others; to be flexible and able to adapt to changing circumstances; to learn to wait until you're in the right frame of mind before making important decisions.

4. **Relationship management.** You try to control people forcefully or you alienate people by your behaviors.

   - **The problem:** You use your control drama to get your way with others.

   - **The solution:** Look for a pattern of behavior when you're trying to manipulate someone to get what you want. There's a difference between negotiation and manipulation. In a negotiation, both sides are satisfied; when you manipulate, you're only concerned with your own needs.

   - **The goal:** To be able to communicate clearly, inspire others, work well in a team, and keep your cool during a conflict.

We do not want to control our emotions to the point that they are repressed and may become debilitative, causing potential harm in the long run, both physically and psychologically.

It is important to note the intensity level and duration of debilitative thoughts and emotions such as fear, hate, frustration, and anger. In fact, most people have felt these emotions at one time or another. We need to learn to cope with irrational or distorted views by stepping back and applying rational emotional therapy to the situation.

Look at the event in question.

- What is your belief regarding that event?
- Is your reaction to that event based on what you believe is going to happen?

If we step back from our emotions, not tying them to any person or event, perhaps empathizing or showing compassion toward another person who may be the trigger for this emotion, we will discover that emotions can, in fact, be managed to the point where they will do a complete turnaround.

- Annoyances can be turned around through understanding.
- Jealousy can be turned around by applying self-love.
- Analyze your reaction in private so as to prevent the same situation from occurring again.

The existence and power of collective consciousness is primordial.

As it relates to emotional intelligence, if we can manage our emotions in such a way as to come from debilitative to facilitative, if laughter and joy, sadness and even indifference are in essence contagious, if we learn by example and redundancy, if we can 'sense' how another person is feeling, I believe that the power of many minds together, all thinking and feeling the same thought, can do great wonders, can influence nations and can change the world.

Guide your thinking, your feelings and your behaviors. Experience them but don't let them control you! Take responsibility for pointing yourself in the right direction.

For this to be successful, you will need to release from responsibility all those people whom you believe have hurt or wronged you in some way. Forget the motivation behind why they did what they did. Just let it go. You will not be weaker for not having confronted them. You will be stronger because you're releasing all the pent up negative energy and making room for positive productive energy.

Honing Your Intuition

If you've been feeling a profound sense of restlessness, this is a good sign. It means you're alert, becoming aware, and paying attention. You're beginning to be more present in your own life. These moments of restlessness will be different from the rest of your day; somehow more intense. They're often accompanied by some sort of inspiration which, when ended, will be followed once again by restlessness and maybe even some dissatisfaction.

That's when you know you're on the right track. Follow those moments of inspiration wherever they may lead. Let your intuition guide you even if it seems a bit out of your comfort zone. You will gain insight that is unknown to you right now. It's like asking a 'why' question. Once you know why, once you know the motivation behind something, you gain insight into how to get to the point of action.

You may run into what seems like a coincidence at these times. For example, you hadn't planned on going to the coffee shop this day but your intuition made you turn the wheel of your car before passing it by. Inside, "coincidentally", there's a book signing going on. You were just wondering how you could get involved in a book signing for your own work. Now is the perfect opportunity to ask this author how to go about it or to simply observe. This type of meaningful interaction happens every single day. They're not few or far between.

Learn to recognize meaningful coincidence. You picked up this book. Every time something like this happens, it should draw you to reconsider the inherent mystery of existence, the "why" things happen and the way they happen. This is a door opening for you as a result of your intention, your decision.

Eventually, your intuition will become a psychological contagion. These events will occur more often and will build a sort of "logic" in your brain. They'll become the dominant imprints; your "perspective filter" will have begun to change.

Answers always come in the present moment. They cannot come in the past or future. The 'coincidences' you attract are part of the collective consciousness of likeminded people, an extension of the Divine mind directed at you.

To gain insight, you must incorporate awareness, mindfulness, presence, paying attention, disciplining your thoughts, thankfulness, appreciation, releasing the past, and taking part in the cycle of giving and receiving.

Practice Ruthless Prioritization

As you go through the steps to discover your why: why you exist, why you want to be, do or have something, why you're passionate about anything in particular, you must practice what I call Ruthless Prioritization. This is what's going to create your path of execution.

What does that mean?

You've discovered who you are at the core, your authentic self. You've found your why: why you want to do, be or have your intended goal. You've learned about the value of leading and living through the lens of Love, including managing your emotions and adding value to the lives of others, and you've learned how to set goals to get where you want to be.

Now you must prioritize your tasks, the things you do every day or need to do to get there. You'll make a Mind Map of the big picture goal and all the tasks that need to take place to achieve that goal.

Eliminate distractions such as partying, watching TV, and hanging out by 80%. They're not priorities and do nothing to move you forward. Your friends may listen to your dreams, but they can't put themselves in your shoes. If you want this bad enough, you need to only do those things that are consistent with keeping you moving forward towards your goal.

You won't know all the steps in the beginning. No one can. You don't know what you don't know. But you should have a plan in place. If you get stuck on something, be flexible and adapt. Find another solution to the little stuff, but don't get stuck on them.

For example, if you intended to attend a seminar about something that would educate you, and the seminar is cancelled, this should not be seen as a setback. Instead, go buy a book, talk to a business owner, find a mentor, or simply reschedule another seminar.

If you're building a prototype for an idea you have, and for some reason, it just doesn't work, don't scrap the idea altogether. Find a work-around. Figure out what went wrong and start again. Just don't give up.

Plans often go wrong. Be flexible. As Mike Tyson said, "Everyone has a plan until they get punched in the mouth." Can You DIGG It? I knew that you could!

Being Present vs. Living on Autopilot

I've talked about how the only moment we have is now, this moment. Nothing can happen in the past or the future. The moment of power is right now. Each second we are blessed with should be filled with positive emotions. Feel that blessing in everything you do and be grateful for what you have NOW!

Remember that time is a man-made concept. It's an illusion. But because our society and therefore our lives are bound to the clock, the illusion has become real.

Beyond what we can currently comprehend about space and time are all the answers to all the secret mysteries of life. And it's there that only one process takes place.

Creation!

Like beautiful old instruments that are collected not played, your gifts are meant to be used, not hidden in the dusty recesses of your mind.

Consciousness is what turns thoughts into things in our objective world, but our experience in this world is always subjective. So whatever we're aware of becomes what we experience and vice versa.

What you create through your awareness becomes what you experience. If you're passive in your thinking, you will still have experiences, but what you experience will not be of your making.

If your experience—what you see in the world, how you act or react, how people treat you, and so on—is not to your liking, understand that it's a direct reflection of you and what you created or allowed someone to create for you because you were passive about your world.

If you've been passive, you've essentially been thwarting your life. This is the irony of the journey, that the universe acts whether you're aware of it or not.

But even when you begin to realize that you are the producer of all that you experience, it can be difficult to turn the switch on when you want to.

Pattern Interrupts

When you're living on autopilot, you simply go through the motions of daily living—getting dressed, eating, brushing your teeth, driving to work--without reflecting on growth, change, and how everything you did that day has affected you and your world. You are not being present for each moment. You are not guiding your thoughts and actions in any particular way. You are simply existing.

These habits or patterns are useful because it makes us efficient at doing mundane tasks, but they can also be detrimental. Eating is a good example of how, if we're not mindful of how and what we're eating, we might overeat, not enjoy food, eat junk just to satisfy a need, and perhaps not eat enough.

There are messages being given to us every day, but because we're living on autopilot, these messages are lost on us. We miss opportunities, meaningful coincidence, and the joy that can be found in being and doing.

Here are some great ways to interrupt the patterns that often control our daily lives:

- Find humor in life. Laugh rather than taking everything so seriously.

- Take a break to relieve stress or anger; go for a walk.

- Change the way you do an everyday task, such as taking a different route to work.

- Take a break from mundane activities such as watching TV. Leave it for at least a few days.

- Take a day to think about creative solutions to a problem rather than becoming frustrated, feeling rushed, or pushing through a decision.

If we can learn to redirect our patterns of behavior and habitual thought, we leave ourselves open to new ideas and ways of doing things. Remember the subconscious mind and how it sees life like a repeating movie? This is what we're talking about here. The subconscious is great at repeating patterns because that's what it knows and it does it automatically.

There is a constant vigilance that must take place in order to 'stay on top of' your awareness and how your experiences, behaviors, and patterns affect your life.

The universe reflects back to you without judgment. The outer world has no power over you and merely gives back without distortion. It's your own perception that distorts and judges. Every perception you have gives rise to a world that mirrors it. Interrupting negative or non-productive patterns (watching TV, losing your temper, non-mindful eating, socializing without listening) will enrich your life by opening the door to opportunity and expose choices you were not aware of.

So living this new truth that you will create is what will make it true. There is no need for stress or drama unless this is what you favor. Every divisive threatening action is a choice you make, and if you are conscious of these choices and make them favorable, you will attain unity.

Once you are in unity with all that is, you cannot harm anyone unless you wish to harm yourself. This is what it means to "be present". You're aware of your thoughts and how they affect you. And whatever affects you affects others.

Everything you can imagine you can achieve. Whatever it is that you seek is already inside you. You already are this person you want to be. Do not apply false assumptions about who you are or what you know. You cannot find something that is outside yourself.

If you are not willing to get off autopilot, you won't know where you're going but you will struggle to get there. Growth can only unfold as you become aware and are ready to receive it.

Don't ever try to follow someone else's map or blueprint for life. Their perception is very different from yours. What is significant to their growth may have no meaning for you.

Awareness of Self: The Nature of Our Next Evolution

Uncompromised faith is something with which many people struggle. We're all plagued at one time or another with sins of the spirit that keep us from our potential and drag us through life with shame, hatred or depression.

The world's religions have played a major role in forming humankind's opinions about everything from what we eat to how we treat ourselves and others. But taking a look beyond reason and religion, taking a step that breaks all religious rules, we find we are in fact spirit itself, without governorship except that which we define within our own souls, the dynamics of which are completely within our control; where space and time are rather irrelevant and the entire purpose of existence is the soul's evolution.

People around the world, from all backgrounds, cultures, and countries, believe there is more that governs life than the mere physicality we see around us. Some believe the doorway to freedom lies in our experiences and the way we choose to use them, while others believe in deeper consciousness, where we must pilot our way, traversing our own wisdom and the wisdom of our personal ancestors until we come to enlightenment of a sort that we can apply to this life.

Humans, after complex evolutionary steps, are now in the next phase, perhaps the final phase: that of recognizing God directly. This is a level of self-awareness or consciousness that gives us the sense of knowing God in ourselves, experiencing what God, the "experiencer", sees. The Universe lives through you!

But evolutionary enlightenment relies on the intuition of the spirit.

The nature of the next evolution of our species is within our direct control if we maintain a proper perspective of our cosmic connection with the origin of our consciousness.

If you're looking for a new way of seeing the universe and how humans "fit in", consider that all human beings are God or a part of the mind of God—part of the whole now separated but not separate.

If you're interested in growing the trinity of mind, body, and spirit into a greater connection to your source, look at how the universe continues to work with us and how we can channel its energy to make our lives better.

- Ground yourself and break through blockages (doubts, fears, shortcomings, and human failings) that are keeping you from your purpose.

- Use pattern interrupts to recognize negative or non-productive habits.

- Get in touch with your inner wisdom and focus on your strengths intuitionally rather than intellectually.

- Be BlessednGrateful™ NOW for what you have and what you are about to receive.

Real life people with honest human experiences, in situations we can all relate to, show us a world in which faith and belief in our own inner power, viewed through the proper lens, is there for all of us to experience.

Can You DIGG It? I knew that you could!

9.

THE SEVENTH POWER: IT: THE POWER OF HAPPINESS

There's no magic formula, no hidden agenda and no miracle except for the miracle which you envision. But your vision for yourself must be backed by the belief that it's achievable.

Real magic doesn't trick you. It makes you believe.

I could not be more blessed or more grateful for the transformation that's occurred in my life, but it never would have happened if I didn't believe it could happen, if I didn't ask for it to happen. You may have heard this before and you may have even tried to apply this to your life, but nothing changed. Why? I can tell you it's because you had baggage that your subconscious mind was holding onto. Your 'stuff' was holding you back, keeping you from really seeing your full potential and from truly believing things could change.

The bottom line is this: you can very likely achieve anything you want to see show up in your life, and you will learn how to do this by reading this book and following the very simple guidelines for getting there. But you will need to do the work. You've already taken the first step by being here. You've already set creation in motion to give you what you need. Your behavior indicates that you are willing to learn, that you want to develop a new self. I've given you the steps to get out of your comfort zone and commit to a new life of reciprocity—getting what you give and giving more than you get. Don't worry. It won't cost you anything but your fear.

Continue to be grateful, particularly after you've 'made it'. Do it every day. Be appreciative of everything because you can just as easily lose what you've gained by not recognizing your blessings. In this way, your successes will become more impressive and greater than you may have imagined by reinforcing the fact that you've succeeded. Internalize all your success. You did it!

Cultivating Happiness

It's possible that we can all agree on one thing: love is transforming. But loving life, loving someone else, and loving yourself don't always come easy for some people.

Does that mean we're doing something wrong? In a way, yes, it does, although that doesn't make you a bad person. Just one who doesn't understand how to cultivate your own happiness through self-love.

One misconception many people hold is that there needs to be an outlet for love, that if there isn't a person willing to receive our love, we cannot properly express it. But love, if you know how to see it and feel it, can be anywhere, and it doesn't need to include another person.

Love and happiness contain energy. If you view life as not being that great, you have the power to change your view about anything and everything, including your view of the people around you.

As soon as you start the process in your mind of moving from where you don't like being towards where you want to be, the love you give to your life comes back to you.

Why is the love you give to the world, your life, yourself, and the people surrounding you the way to happiness?

Love is energy, but how do you feel that energy and how can you work with it?

How do you find and identify the love within yourself and try to enrich it?

We live in a world where everyone has an opinion and the resources to express it, but opinions don't matter to the truth.

Perhaps you're judgmental; you look at your world with preconceived notions about how things should be, and when they don't turn up that way or when someone falls short of your expectations, you judge their behavior by your own standards, by what you would have done.

Learning to love means accepting people the way they are and finding something good in them or about them, regardless of whether or not you actually like them.

When you get in the habit of assuming the best, good things generally find their way to you. Happiness is a decision. You can be as happy as you decide to be.

Here are 16 tips that will truly enrich your life so you can experience more happiness.

1. **Listen to Your Heart**

   It's very easy to become distracted by all the things we need to get done in a day or a week, but you must make time for yourself.

   - What do you enjoy doing?

   - Who do you feel happy being around?

   - Which people in your life don't make you feel good about yourself?

   - Be aware of all the little things that make you uncomfortable.

   - Really listen to what your intuition is telling you.

   - Don't ignore your gut feelings.

   - Be mindful of everything around you and how you feel so you will recognize all the little things that contribute to your happiness.

2. **Stay Positive**

   - Stop looking at everything negatively.

   - Don't be a hater.

   - Be happy for the abundance and good fortune of others. Your joy over someone else's success will come back to you tenfold.

   - Continue to find something that makes you happy, even if only for a day. Keep the energy around you positive by surrounding yourself with happy people.

   - Don't let others drain you with their constant complaining or bad attitudes.

   - Treat yourself to a coffee or lunch out.

- Pursue what makes you happy. And don't be thinking about all the things you need to get done. Just enjoy whatever it is you're doing now.

3. **Drop the Frenzy**

   - Is it possible to stay off social media for just one day? For just a few hours? Can you drop just one thing from your to-do Map that isn't really all that important or pressing?

   - Stop your mind if only for a few minutes. Just sit in a chair without TV, phones or music and listen to the quiet.

   - Don't be attached to outcomes. If you plan to go on a picnic and it rains, plan it for another day or find a spot that's under cover and enjoy your picnic while you watch the rain!

   - And do it without advertising where you are on Twitter, Facebook, or via phone.

4. **Find the Humor in Everything**

   Life is full of challenges, but it's also full of opportunities.

   - Keep everything in perspective, and when you feel like you're ready to rumble, find something humorous in the situation.

   - There's a reason for everything and a purpose for what you may be going through, but you won't see that reason or purpose if you're angry, judgmental, and resentful.

   - Humor heals and relaxes and allows you to view life from a different perspective.

5. **Relax and Breathe**

   This goes hand in hand with humor, positivity, and dropping the frenzy. Learning to relax is one of the best things you can do for yourself when it comes to self-love. I have my phone alarm set to remind me to take 3 deep breaths every 2 hours!

- Care about yourself, how you feel, what you want, and who you allow into your life.

- Thinking about this when you're in a relaxed state will make everything clearer.

- Don't hate the people and things that are negative in your life. Just embrace the positive instead.

- Breathe in good energy and say 'no' to anything that feels like resistance.

6. **Assume the Best**

We all want to place the blame on someone or something when things don't go our way.

- If a plan doesn't come together because someone dropped the ball, assume they had a good reason for doing so and that they were doing the best they could at the moment.

- Just learn from it and move on.

- If you are the reason for not making something happen, take responsibility.

- Recognizing where you went wrong and adjusting, being flexible, will go a long way to continuing happiness.

- It's ok to make mistakes, but always assume the best, always give the benefit of the doubt unless something proves otherwise. This is part of staying positive.

7. **Have No Regrets**

   We all make mistakes and can regret things we've done or never got around to doing. Don't allow your past—the very thing your subconscious mind feeds on—dictate your present.

   They say you can't change your past, but in a way you can. Simply change your perception of it. Turn it into a positive in some way. That way your mind sees this as a good experience, something you've learned from. In the future, you will not feel badly when you think of the mistakes you may have made.

8. **Face Your Fears**

   Get to the root cause of your fear. If you have stage fright or a fear of public speaking, were you laughed at or forgot your lines in the high school play? If you're afraid of heights, is this an unreasonable fear?

   Understand why you're afraid and then release that fear. That doesn't mean you have to climb to the top of the Empire State Building or scale Mount Kilimanjaro. Just let go of fear and you will be happier.

9. **Maintain Your Integrity**

   If you're not happy with yourself, you won't be happy with anything or anyone else. Everyone has a moral code of conduct and values they were raised with or developed as adults. Don't allow yourself to be swayed from this.

   If friends don't agree with you, that's ok. You don't need to sulk over it. Just stay happy and let them live their lives according to how they see it.

10. **Be Generous**

There are many ways to be generous that don't involve money. Having a generosity of spirit is one of the most selfless things a person can do. Be kind, have a good word to say, bestow honest compliments, give of your time if possible, allow someone else to take the credit or be in the limelight.

11. **Lose Control**

We've all met control freaks; people who can't let the smallest thing go by without giving their opinion on how it should be done or trying to make others do things their way. When their control is threatened, they can become ill-tempered.

Allow yourself to lose your controlling nature. Let the kids get dirty; leave the dishes in the sink overnight; allow your husband to watch the game on Sunday instead of mowing the lawn. You only get to control one life: your own.

Another way people maintain control is by never allowing themselves to be imperfect. Play like a child. Forget about who's watching. Laugh and be silly. Eat off your diet.

12. **Nurture Your Own Soul**

Some people feel they need to have a significant other to be happy. But if you wait around for that someone to appear, you may be waiting a long time, or you may settle just so you're not alone.

Don't count on others for your happiness. Get out (or stay in) and do the things that bring you joy. And don't do them while thinking about how much better they would be if someone else were with you.

13. **Drop Expectations**

We often put others on a pedestal, particularly those we love. But putting them up there means we expect a lot from them, and this can often lead to disappointment.

Allow people to live their lives according to their own conscience. Give them room to breathe. That doesn't mean you shouldn't have standards, just don't expect everyone else to live by them.

14. **Trust Yourself**

As an adult, you should know your own mind. Follow your instincts and your gut. Don't doubt yourself. And don't put yourself down.

Use positive self-talk if you have an issue with esteem. Don't ask others if you look okay, if they like your new haircut, or if they like what you're wearing. If you like it, that's good enough. If you don't like it, having someone think you look okay is probably not going to change how you feel about yourself.

15. **View Life Objectively**

The human mind experiences things subjectively. In other words, our experiences are unique to us. How we view an experience as it happens determines our reaction to it.

Keep an open mind. Don't allow jealousy or envy into your life. View everything from the perspective of someone who has nothing to gain or lose from the situation. In this way, you'll be able to consciously determine your action rather than letting your subconscious mind do it based on your past experiences.

16. **Keep a Positive Attitude**

When it comes to happiness, this should really go without saying. Your thoughts and words influence your feelings, which influence those around you. The energy you give is reflected back to you.

If you get stuck in a negative dump, remove yourself mentally from the thoughts that are causing them. Find something positive to do temporarily. Then you can revisit those negative thoughts and it will be easier to figure out what caused them; why you reacted the way you did.

So perception plays a huge part in your ability to stay happy. Your subconscious mind perceives things based on your past similar experiences and reacts, or causes you to react, in the same old way.

By changing your perception of everything that makes you unhappy, you can reverse your world and be happy all the time. Then if someone puts a fly in your ointment, it will only be a short temporary stay.

Everyone Has an Excuse

We all have excuses and some of them are valid. But you'll have to work through and around them, no matter what they are. Resistance to change won't get you what you want. Besides, there's absolutely nothing to be afraid of.

"In a chronically leaking boat, energy devoted to changing vessels is more productive than energy devoted to patching leaks."

-Warren Buffett

So let's take it from the beginning.

You've committed yourself to doing this. You've obtained the book and you're actually reading it. I'm very happy for you.

You've been looking into how to get what you want, and you've now heard of the Law of Attraction. It's been around for thousands of years but only in recent history has it been developed into a science and termed this way.

Countless free thinkers, entrepreneurs, and visionaries have used this concept. Many have developed their own interpretations of it using different methods that entail the same core fundamentals. And while experience, intelligence, and knowledge all play a part, your successes and your failures don't happen specifically because of them in the way you might believe they do.

What you believe becomes your experience which serves to strengthen your belief which in turn reinforces your experience. Your intelligence analyzes your experience and validates your beliefs while this "knowledge" becomes ingrained in you.

The knowledge you received as a child needs to be reprogrammed. This is what needs to change. One of the biggest things you'll have to do is let go. Let go of the past and everything you learned about success. Let go of the how and the why. Don't try to figure out how something is going to happen for you. Simply begin to focus on the goal itself.

Resistance to change, however, is a funny thing. As soon as we decide we're going to do something, all this resistance comes boiling up along with the excuses that try to make that resistance valid. That's why the Law of Resistance is labeled as one of the natural laws of life. It hits us all at some time or other. For example, from the time we're kids, we resist going to sleep even though we can't keep our eyes open.

Most of the successful people in the world are no smarter that you are. They have no more common sense than you and their education may not necessarily be greater.

So what exactly do they have that you don't? They possess the right kind of experience and knowledge of how the world works.

They applied the 7 Can You DIGG It? powers which encompass the God-given Law(s) of Attraction and Abundance to get what they wanted.

- Can: Beliefs: Everything they desired was made to happen because they believed it would happen. "There is no man living that cannot do more than he thinks he can." (Henry Ford)

- You: "The strongest force in the Universe is a human being living consistently with his identity." (Tony Robbins)

- D - Decide: "Once you make a decision, the Universe conspires to make it happen." (Ralph Waldo Emerson)

- I - Imagination: "If you can dream it, you can do it." (Walt Disney)

- G - Go: "You don't have to be great to start, but you have to start to be great." (Zig Ziglar)

- G - Guidance: "Self-control is the quality that distinguishes the fittest to survive." (George Bernard Shaw)

- It - Happiness: "The purpose of our lives is to be happy!" (Dalai Lama)

That's why, to the uninitiated, it seems as though there are the lucky few who achieve success time and time again. What these "lucky few" have learned, based on their prior experiences, is that the methods they've employed have yielded results. They'd be foolish to stray from a system that works so they repeat it for more successes. Can you DIGG It? I knew that you could!

What, exactly, is the idea behind this? It bears repeating.

The energy you put out into the world - your thoughts, emotions, and actions - everything you believe, is returned to you in a mirror image.

Successful people made their own luck by preparing for the moment when they could seize an opportunity which might move them in the direction of what they wanted.

Wishing for something you want is a fantasy. Believing you'll get something, that you deserve it, that you'll do everything necessary to get it, is locked within the power of your intention.

"In the universe there is an immeasurable indescribable force which shamans call intent, and absolutely everything that exists in the entire cosmos is attached to intent by a connecting link."

- Carlos Castaneda

Wayne Dyer, motivational speaker and author of more than 30 books on the subject, affectionately known as the "father of motivation", believed we have to let go and just allow. We have to be free and make this our consciousness. "Basically, what you would see is a frequency (of energy) that manifests itself through the process of giving, of allowing, of offering, and of serving. It asks nothing back."

"Ask and it will be given to you; seek and you will find; knock and the door will be opened to you." Matthew 7:7 NIV

The Bible is thousands of years old, so you can see that this is not a new idea, however ancient traditions and methods which have long been forgotten still work for the modern world. But in the words of Napoleon Hill, there's a difference between asking and being ready to receive. If you follow through with your affirmations and everything else you know of to get where you want to be, you'll be ready to receive, and as you do, new doors and opportunities will open for you.

The reason people don't get what they want is because they don't ask for it, they don't know how to ask for it. They just don't DIGG It yet.

If you take an active part in pursuing your goals, the world interprets this as you having faith in and believing that what you want is out there for you. You've set your frequency to the same frequency as that which you are about to receive.

You must be persistent and repetitive with your affirmation, not because you are trying to convince God or the Universe, but because you are trying to reprogram your own thoughts. The Universal mind of God is already prepared to give you what you deserve. By reprogramming your thoughts and intentions using the 7 powers of the Can You DIGG It system, you'll be ready to receive.

- Set in motion the steps you know you can take. You will most likely not foresee the next steps until they are presented to you after completing the first steps.

- Appreciate and express gratitude for everything along the way.

- Remove all negativity and doubt.

- Do not try to hide or subdue your past, but look at the source of your fears.

"Do that which is assigned to you... and in that moment you will be as brave as the pen of Moses."

- Ralph Waldo Emerson

Continue to be BlessedNGrateful™, particularly after you've reached IT! Don't stop being BlessednGrateful™, don't stop guiding your thoughts after you've started DIGGin' your life. When you're Loving your Life, keep that energy going! Do it every day. Be appreciative of everything because you can just as easily lose what you've gained by not recognizing your blessings. In this way, your successes will become more impressive and greater than you may have imagined by reinforcing the fact that you've succeeded. Internalize all your success. You did it! Your mind actually expects this now rather than expecting resistance, fear and failure.

When you become successful, there's always a chance that you'll feel guilty because you now have more than your family or close friends. You want to bring them up with you. We're all worthy of receiving great things, so if you can help others, do so by all means. But don't get to the point where you take on the burden of anyone who is not willing to do the work for themselves. Buy them a copy of this book. Have them connect with me at john-diggs.com. I'm very happy to do a Free Mind Map with them through one of my webinars.

Your Power to Impact Others

From the time we're old enough to understand language, we're bribed with toys or sweets to make us stop crying or behave in a certain way. We're shown what appears to be love; we're cooed at, given a pat on the shoulder, talked at, and even scolded. But the reality of these actions is that they are merely a means of trying to make us conform to whatever it is our parents, guardians, teachers, and friends need from us. They need us to stop crying, stop craving and stop wanting them to show us the affection and love that has been effectively drummed out of them since they were children.

"If you don't miss a day of school, I will buy you that new pair of shoes." "If you don't cry anymore, I will give you a lollipop." We might read this and chuckle, but it's what has been stunting the spiritual and intellectual growth of humans across the board.

So what's the solution?

The Spirit is the animating force traditionally believed to be within living beings, sometimes referred to as the soul, intangible and believed by some to be independent from the physical body in nature. It's generally regarded as immortal.

While the body is completely measurable and the mind is the newest horizon for studying the measurability and therefore the potential of humankind, the spirit or soul is intangible - we cannot reach it by any measurable standard or technology.

Yet if you have ever been in love or felt compassion or a deep connection to a loved one, especially as experienced after the death of the loved one, you are aware of your essence, your spirit, your soul.

Love cannot be seen or measured by science. Yet brainwaves have shown a significant difference in subjects who were tested after having watched a sad movie and a love story. The effects of love can be measured but not love itself, yet most of us would agree it exists. How then can we agree that something exists if we cannot measure it or sense it in the physical way, using the five physical senses?

We agree that it exists because we believe that it exists. We feel that it exists in an unexplainable and immeasurable way. And therefore, we know that it exists. And it's this type of knowing that is the foundation for all the God-given natural laws of the universe.

So, again, what's the solution?

Whether we're talking about friends, family, business relationships or even just acquaintances, the answer is non-judgmental love. And you can't give this to others if you don't have it for yourself.

- Forgive yourself for all the real or imagined slights you think you are responsible for.

- Show real emotions. They won't diminish you or make you weak.

- Don't be afraid to be vulnerable.

- Drop the mask that 'gets you through the day'.

- Try to pinpoint the learned behaviors that might be holding you back from being your authentic self.

- Stop looking for 'safety' in relationships. It's good to feel safe in a relationship, but don't make it the reason for starting or staying in one.

- Don't place conditions on giving your love. "I will love you if you do this."

- Ask yourself "What will happen if I drop my guard?"

Non-judgmental love is not a feeling, it's an action. You decide to be non-judgmental in the same way you decide to love in the first place. Adding value in the form of non-judgmental love to your management style is something that will bring great returns for you and your team. You are adding value to the world and this will be paid back tenfold by those who receive it.

"Stand firm… be men of courage. Do everything in love."
(1 Corinthians 16:13, 14)

Are you the kind of person who wants to succeed but doesn't want to feel any pain or make any effort? Don't give in to negativity, discouragement, or others telling you that you can't do something. Develop your work ethic and your personal relationship skills. Continue to be present and listen to others. Stay connected and ask yourself, "What if I could institute a change in this person's life? How would my own life be affected if I could do this?"

It's okay to want more, but in the final analysis, be BlessednGrateful™. Be BlessednGrateful™. for everything you have regardless of how much or how little: your money, your clients, your sales, your wardrobe, your team, your family and friends, your time off, your car, your weight – all of it. This will always bring a smile to your face, and what you project is reflected back to you.

Success does not bring happiness. Happiness brings success.

Don't spend your life complaining about how you've tried and failed or about all the things you want and don't have. Do what you need to do to lay the groundwork for what you want. Realize that your power is inborn. Don't look to the outside world to create it for you.

The human brain remembers by reinforcement and repetition.

The way you "see" your world will be the world that will take shape for you. In exactly the same way that repetitive reinforcement made you what you are today, it can change you into what you want to be. Every time you think about something - anything - it begins to imprint on your brain. The more you think about it, the more you brain remembers it.

The pictures you "store" in your mind will play back like movies, causing you to think about them further and the message is reinforced. So whether you're saying "I'm ugly" or "I'm receiving more wealth", the effect will be the same. This is what you'll begin to believe because this is how the human mind works.

Once you begin to believe it, you'll begin to attract whatever is necessary to make that happen. You'll meet the right people who can show you more right people; you'll be the right person in the right place at the right time.

It's a great feeling to know that the system is working equally for everyone. Fall in love with being part of that. Even if you only believe something in your wildest dreams, it will start to manifest for you if it's what you intend. Make sure your actions don't contradict your desires.

Focused self-awareness, your most focused thought, can literally alter human biology. I know this. I've made it happen for me. I saved my own life through the power of God's given Laws of Nature: the Laws of Attention, Attraction, Action, Compensation, Projection, Perpetual Transmutation of Energy, Reciprocity, and the Law of Divine Oneness.

Life and health, knowledge, and harmony are desirable for everyone. I smile a lot and I'm often asked why I smile so much. It's because I live by the basic belief that we have been given the power to create our own lives through mindful intention and the recognition that our energy is malleable, not fixed. In short, I Can DIGG It!

Live your life in the pursuit of justice and compassion, with interrelated love for all things. Humankind is at the tip of consciousness evolution.

You are not right, you are not first, you are not individual, but that type of thinking informs how you operate and separates you from love.

There is no separation or competition between us, just a need for unconditional love. This is the key to understanding our connection, that which binds us to each other and to the Creator.

I hope I've given you enough information to change your life by:

- Believing you are a Spiritual Being, blessed with the ability to decide how you want to experience life.

- Understanding that you are what you say you are, not what you've been conditioned to believe.

- Having a conscious perception of the vibration you are putting out there, an awareness of what and how you're thinking.

- Understanding that you can create the life you love by imagining yourself experiencing that life, taking action, and guiding yourself towards your desires until you achieve happiness.

Infinite Wisdom has granted us all the tools we need, the Laws which are unwavering and given in equal amount to any who will ask.

We all have within us the power to change the conditions of our lives, to live without lack, want, doubt, fear, struggle, pain, and sorrow; to demonstrate the blessings and abundance provided for us. Nothing happens by chance. The Law of Divine Oneness states that we are all interconnected.

I want to congratulate you for DIGGin' this project.

You were born with Divine consciousness.

10.

INTERNAL TRANSFORMATION

Once you have gone through and mastered the 7 Powers, you will have changed what you believe about yourself and your abilities; you will have identified your authentic self and decided what you desire most; you will have learned to make the right decisions based on what you now believe to be possible and you'll guide your gift through your imagination, inspiration, thoughts, and intention. You've begun to take the required action to achieve your vision.

You've reached the point of internal transformation. This will manifest as pure Happiness! This is what you'll feel when you achieve your goals and realize your dreams. This is what happens when we reach our ultimate goal of Loving Life!

The words transformation and change are often used interchangeably, and although the definitions of these words may sound similar, their meanings, applications, and outcomes are very different.

The Difference Between Change and Transformation

This entire book is about transforming yourself so you can achieve what you desire most and Love Life. But transformation is not about the physical, although that may be a pleasant side effect of this process.

Change is caused by outside or external influences. The lunch room menu was changed. The steak was changed to hamburger. The team implemented changes to the plays. Uniforms were changed to include short-sleeved shirts. The weather changed from rain to snow.

Think about computer program changes. They're put in place, but they don't stay that way. Someone needs to maintain and manage processes that continually optimize them. They involve metrics and algorithms that are constantly being improved. So there's this external effort that's required to achieve the necessary results. Change can be small or on a large scale, but it always requires some external force or influence.

Transformation almost always takes place on a large scale. It's significant to how you view life or perform actions. It occurs when your beliefs and why you do what you do has undergone change. But this change has taken place within you.

It's everything I've been talking about I this book.

If you want to transform your beliefs and the way you view your world, you must focus on yourself. This is what awareness is. It's not a selfish "me first" attitude. It's about understanding why you are the way you are and how you became that way. What caused you to become or believe what you do?

You must commit to this; to continually trying to improve and understand yourself, your motivations, and the reason behind your actions.

This is a good place for me to quickly go through what you'll experience as you go from the first power, the Power of Beliefs, to the seventh power, the Power of Happiness.

I'm putting this near the end of the book because, if you've read this far, you will soon be implementing all the powers. At least I hope that you will. And you need to know what to expect.

The Four Stages of Transformation

Throughout this process, you'll be discovering new ways of thinking, listening, and seeing yourself and your world. Everyone is different. There are multiple answers to multiple questions. One size definitely does not fit all.

Welcome to the matrix, where you'll transform into authenticity; where you'll drop the drumbeats of the past, and where you'll see beyond the linear to a world that does not yet exist.

But it will!

Right now you're deeply rooted in the experience of your traditional thinking, and that's the basis for your life as you know it. Now it's time to disrupt everything and take a different approach. The old ways don't work for you anymore. You may not be able to predict exactly what will happen, and that's why you must be willing to remain flexible.

When life throws you a curve ball, as it inevitably will, just reassess your position, your plan, your strategy. Create a work-around. Evolve and adapt and pay attention to your life as never before. Be mindful of every thought and action.

You're going to go through the four phases of transformation - analyzing, understanding, risking, and continuing to evolve until you reach IT. You are going to remain focused on the big picture outcome, but you are going to apply maniacal flexibility and creativity in the execution path.

There are essentially four stages you'll go through before you reach transformation.

1. **The Resistance**
2. **The Fence**
3. **The Awakening**
4. **The Yes!**

Let's begin with the toughest stage to get through.

The Resistance

I think it's fairly safe to say that not too many people actually like change. Even if they are forced to make changes, they rarely embrace them. They resist it at every turn. This is particularly true when we're talking about the human personality.

Few people are actually willing to take a good look at themselves and notice their own flaws. And even fewer are willing to do anything about those flaws. So resistance becomes the number one obstacle to transformation. But if you resist, if you don't want to change anything about yourself and the way you do things, if you remain stuck in the old ways and beliefs, it's unlikely you'll be able to see your way to success beyond your wildest dreams.

The Fence

This is the stage where you might actually be thinking, "Hmmm, there might be something to this whole process. It makes sense even if I don't quite buy into it totally yet. I'll keep an open mind." Good for you.

The Awakening

Now is when you that lightbulb will go off in your head and you'll say, "Aha! I'm starting to get it. I'm starting to see things differently. I'm beginning to understand how this can actually work for me." Each step you take that's consistent with your goals will bring you closer to that "Aha" moment. And eventually, you'll get to...

The Yes!

You now see that you were the obstacle all along. You and what you believed about yourself and everything around was the reason you could not move forward; the reason you could not even comprehend of a better life for yourself outside of a fantasy.

You've taken it one step at a time, broken through your resistance, visualized the life you want, set your goals, held yourself accountable, tracked your progress, rolled with the punches, learned from your mistakes, and surrounded yourself with like-minded individuals.

Internal Transformation results in The Power of Happiness. Once you change what you Believe about yourself, find your Authentic Self, Decide what you want to do, Imagine yourself doing that and find the Inspiration to do it, Get Going and take Action. Guide your thoughts and your Gifts consistently in the direction of your goals: what you want to be, do, and have. You must keep prioritizing until you have those things you've decided you want. When you have IT, you'll have successfully created your Happiness and you'll Love Life! Can You DIGG It? I knew that you could!

Realizing your dream and achieving your goals feels awesome. It's an addicting feeling that you'll surely want to continue.

Eastern Philosophy and the Distinction of Context

The concept of transformation expands on traditional Eastern philosophy regarding the process of enlightenment, giving it a concrete form in our minds rather than an esoteric understanding.

It illuminates the necessity of:

- recognition and distinction of context and its relevance to world views

- shifting states of consciousness

- recognizing how the mind takes on the attributes of that of which we are aware, with our reality becoming observer created

There are endless possibilities for what is, for seeing, knowing, and being.

The messages we receive as we go through our busy lives come from many sources, but not many people pay close attention to the messages that come from intuition or spirit. Instead, we tend to 'read into' what we hear and see, justifying things to fit our needs, our world view, and our experience.

We use our eyes and ears but not our soul to see and hear.

Like any endeavor, if we are to excel at it, we must first go through preparedness and learn to master the idiosyncrasies of the path we choose. And it can be a path where nothing is as it seems on the surface.

Learn to trust that which is unexplainable, not defined by the parameters of your usual course of living. There's much more to living than just the passage of time.

Is Spiritual Growth Spontaneous?

Keep your mind free and experience teachings from all directions. Listen to those teachings which bring progress to your spiritual growth and allow yourself to remain open to changes you're experiencing in yourself.

This is not about self-improvement. It's about freeing yourself from the boundaries of your dogmatic ideas and fixed ways. These are limitations that you must be willing to give up.

There is no timetable for doing this either. Time is another limitation. But you must be disciplined and involved in order to keep your vision before you. You're not waiting for a miracle. You are being proactive in your spiritual journey by reading, observing, listening, and gleaning from those sources who can teach you.

But do not idolize your teachers.

You are meant to be free and your own master. This is what awareness offers. Being your own master does not mean you are right in everything you say and do. That is ego. If ego is your master, you are not free.

Freedom is limitless. If you follow the flow of what brings you the most joy, you will have found a reliable guide into the future, where you will be, do, and have what you desire. In this way your desire and your purpose are linked. When you follow your heart's desire, your purpose will reveal itself. But remember, this can only take place in the present moment.

I would like to point out again and make it very clear that we must keep imagining ourselves succeeding, taking action, and guiding ourselves until we get "It". This is the root of the entire process. Can You DIGG It? I knew that you could!

The Optimist's Creed

The Optimist's Creed was originally published in 1912 in a book titled Your Forces and How to Use Them by Christian D. Larson. I really think it's worth repeating here because it hits the mark in every respect regarding how we can change our lives through the power of thought and the God-given Laws of the Universe, so Please - DIGG this:

Promise Yourself...

To be so strong that nothing can disturb your peace of mind.

To talk health, happiness, and prosperity to every person you meet.

To make all your friends feel that there is something worthwhile in them.

To look at the sunny side of everything and make your optimism come true.

To think only of the best, to work only for the best, and to expect only the best.

To be just as enthusiastic about the success of others as you are about your own.

To forget the mistakes of the past and press on to the greater achievements of the future.

To wear a cheerful expression at all times and give a smile to every living creature you meet.

To give so much time to improving yourself that you have no time to criticize others.

To be too large for worry, too noble for anger, too strong for fear, and too happy to permit the presence of trouble.

To think well of yourself and to proclaim this fact to the world, not in loud words, but in great deeds.

To live in the faith that the whole world is on your side, as long as you are true to the best that is in you.

I'm down, set, and ready to achieve my next goal, to productively use my experience to impact others who are thirsty for help to break through emotional blocks and rid themselves of their time-bound past and anything else that might be keeping them from truly Loving Life!

I'm John Diggs and I'm BlessednGrateful™ to you for allowing me to come into your life through this book. I'm Loving Life and on a Mission to doing all I can to help you Love Life as well!

Can You DIGG It? I knew that you could!

11.

LOVE LIVE! CAN YOU DIGG IT? QUESTIONS

I've designed the following questions for those who have successfully completed reading this book and are implementing the Power tools I've laid out. These questions will serve as a reminder of what you've been through. They will keep you in gratitude and help you continue on any path you choose. They will remind you that Happiness and Loving Life is a simple as changing the thoughts that ruminate in your mind and the actions you take.

Read them whenever you're feeling out of sorts or overwhelmed. They'll keep you on track and remind you that you have created your own success, your own future, and your own life.

- Stay connected to me at **johndiggs.com** and social media

- Sign up for one of my **Free Mind Mapping Webinars**!

- Sign up for my **Can You DIGG It? Newsletter**!

- Look for my **DIGGable Thoughts!**

I'm here to help you sort out anything that's keeping you from Loving Life!

Questions:

CAN

- When did you first believe you could achieve?
- How did that believe come about?
- What happened to reinforce that belief?

YOU

- Who are you?
- When did you begin to see yourself as Spirit living a human experience?
- What is the best part of you? Why do you believe that?

DECISION

- When did you decide to become?
- Why did you decide to become who you are?
- How did you make the decision?

IMAGINATION

- Did you see yourself being who you are today back then?
- How did you see yourself?
- What do you feel when you see yourself? How does that feel?

GO

- What actions did you take?

- How did you determine what actions to take?

- How do you define faith? How does it feel?

GUIDE

- How did you guide your thoughts, feelings and behaviors over the years? How do you guide them now?

- How did you stay focused?

- How has your perspective of your past changed?

- Do you still have fears or worry about the future?

- How do you stay present, aware of what's going on around you right now?

IT

- Can you see how you have transformed internally from a place of chaos, fear, and worry to one of happiness and a 'can-do' attitude?

- What does Loving Life mean to you?

- What topic would you say was the most important to understand?

- How do you define Happiness?

APPENDIX I: LEARNING TO BREATHE

"For breath is life, and if you breathe well, you will live long on Earth."

- Sanskrit Proverb

For most of us, breathing has become an incomplete, superficial and sometimes hasty procedure.

The action of breathing is a powerful driving force in circulation. It moves oxygen deeply through the bloodstream. If you have a sedentary job or lifestyle, you've likely developed congestion in one organ or another. With complete breathing, the bloodstream in organs is prevented from slowing down to the point where it stagnates and degenerates from "stream" to "marsh".

Here's a description of how breathing can work to move blood:

When you breathe in, blood is moved through every tissue in the body. The optimum interchange of gases in the lungs, the absorption of oxygen and the giving off of carbon dioxide, is at its most efficient when breathing is deep, complete and slow.

The large vein continuously pouring blood from the liver into the heart is emptied regularly through suction developed by the lungs in breathing. When the venous blood from the liver can't circulate freely, it becomes congested and causes repercussions throughout the body.

I have my phone alarm set to remind me to take 3 deep cleansing breaths every hour.

It's best to practice proper breathing lying down until you get the feel for it.

- First remove any article of clothing or jewelry that will constrict your neck, chest, lungs, belly, or diaphragm.

- Lie on your back on a firm surface (not your bed).

- Legs should be straight and arms comfortably down along your sides, palms up and elbows gently tucked near the waist.

- Tuck your shoulder blades under to lift your chest a bit and open up your rib cage.

- Do not arch the neck or tuck the head or chin. Your head should be in a natural position with chin pointed toward the opposite wall.

- If necessary, place a low soft pillow under your knees to diminish the lumbar arch.

- Closing your eyes will help you concentrate.

- Relax all the organs and muscles designed to hold things in or hold you up.

1. **Exhale first through your nose.**

   Until a receptacle is empty, it cannot be filled, so in the act of respiration, a slow and complete exhalation is an absolute prerequisite of correct and complete inhalation.

Slowly and calmly exhale through your nose, forcing all air out of your lungs. The chest is depressed by its own weight, expelling air. This out-breath must be slow. At the end of the expiration, use your abdominal muscles to force remaining air out. To do this, pull your abdominal muscles inward, in a contraction toward your back to expel the last traces of tainted air. Because the spongy nature of the lungs does not allow them to fully empty, they will always retain some impure air. You're attempting to minimize that residue.

2. **Breathe in through your nose.**

   Fill your lungs with air. Fill the diaphragm first, then the chest. You're not attempting to blow yourself up like a balloon. Breathe easily, slowly and silently. Think about the action of your lungs, rib cage, diaphragm, clavicle, and intestines as they rise and lower. You may need to yawn. This is a good sign, showing that your lungs are relaxed.

3. **Hold inspiration (in-breath) for 5-20 seconds.**

   When you breathe deeply, the surface of the tiny air sacs (alveoli) in your lungs is increased. All the normally inactive alveoli, unused in everyday breathing, are brought into service. When air remains in contact with lung alveoli, you receive the maximum degree of aeration.

4. **Putting it all together.**

   Lie on your back, exhale through your nose and inhale through your nose. Begin breathing slowly and deeply from your diaphragm.

   - When you feel that it's impossible to raise your diaphragm any more, expand your ribs and allow more air to enter your lungs.

- Once the ribs are fully extended, raise your collar bones so a little more air can enter. Remember, don't try to blow yourself up like a balloon. The whole process should be easy and comfortable. Avoid tensing your hands, face and neck.

- For this practice, hold the in-breath for 5-20 seconds and then slowly release air through the nose for a slow count of 5. When you reach 5, force the air from your lungs using the abdomen to press out remaining air.

- Allow two short ordinary breaths before beginning again.

- Repeat 3 times.

There's a natural immunity attributed to the ionic balance in the blood that, in great part, depends on breathing. This exercise will teach you to focus on the diaphragm rather than primarily using the chest in shallow breathing, which is the way many people breathe on a daily basis.

Learning to breathe properly will also help you during your meditations. You will be more relaxed and able to focus on your intentions

APPENDIX II:
LEARNING TO MEDITATE
& BINAURAL BEATS

Learning to meditate is another strategy to help you stay on track and keep the Thought Police out of your head. What is the connection between meditation and getting what you want? And why should you meditate?

First, let's talk about what meditation is.

By definition, meditation is simply the act of focusing deeply, in silence, as a method of relaxing the mind so as to 'get in touch' with inner consciousness, thereby leading to self-discovery, self-renewal, and spiritual growth.

Traditional meditation often involves a spiritual component. Those who have been practicing it for many years are beyond any self-indulgence, learning self-love, or contemplating daily encounters. Their goal is to connect with God and to understand and be one with all things.

You may wish to take this far or you may only want to use meditation as a means of getting in touch with your own consciousness and how it plays a part in your behavior, the way you view yourself and your world, and as a tool for helping with your visualization. The patterns your mind has set up for you can more easily be changed when you learn to meditate deeply and you will often find answers to perplexing questions.

When you're deep in meditation, you have the opportunity to connect with that part of yourself that is overshadowed during daily waking hours, when everything is about time schedules and the hustle and bustle of everyday activities. You are in silence, within and without; you feel and acknowledge any emotion that arises.

This is where you will meet the Point of Power; this is where you can guide your thoughts, change your beliefs, and visualize your future. It's a good idea to think about what you want to meditate on before you go into relaxation.

Learning to meditate is simple.

Choose a time when you can sit quietly for a designated period, when you will not be disturbed or distracted.

Sit quietly in a relaxed position. Be sure you aren't so comfortable that you fall asleep! An upright chair works well, or you can sit on a mat or towel on the floor with your back straight.

Cross your legs or extend them in a relaxed position. Your hands and arms can fall at your side or you can rest them on your thighs or knees.

Close your eyes and take a few deep breaths in and out through your nose. Try to breathe from the diaphragm not just the upper chest. (See Appendix I: Learning to Breathe.) Envision a place between your eyebrows. This is where the legendary 'third eye' is located. Focus on this spot.

You might hear outside noises, such as a car passing. Let it pass and return your focus to your breathing. Give a visual component to your breath. Assign it a color and watch it move smoothly in through your nose, filling your lungs, and then moving freely out through your nose. (Blue is a good color to use because it represents peace and cooperation).

As you begin to unwind, do not think about anything in particular. Your objective is to relax and 'see' the inner workings of your subconscious mind. Remain in the moment; don't let your mind wander.

The process of meditation follows a particular order. By following your breath, you will get into a rhythm that supports a relaxed mind. The mind is cleared, the body and mind are calmed, and the focus is inward, to the consciousness, not on the external world. When you reach a state of contemplation where you are no longer distracted by what's outside you, your meditation will deepen.

Meditation will enhance creativity and give you keener intuition, deeper sleep, heightened awareness, lower blood pressure, more pronounced insight, and general well-being. With continued practice, you will start to see progressively greater results in your personal and professional life.

Most people limit themselves. They frown on meditation as being some Eastern religion which might interfere with their own personal religious practices and beliefs. But meditating is for everyone, no matter what your religious beliefs.

Meditation and prayer can and should be used together. When you are quiet and relaxed, you can freely and openly talk with the Creator, ask for what you want, express gratitude, and seek guidance.

During meditation, you are conscious and awake, aware of your surroundings but able to 'tune them out'. Because of this heightened awareness, the subconscious takes its cue to make the change you are focused on, and in a short time, it will begin to carry over to your normal everyday state of mind. It will see this as a projection of what you are and will be reinforced each time you go deep into meditation.

You will be more aware about almost everything, and you will grow spiritually and personally. Remember, we are spirits having a human experience who have been subjected to an onslaught of negativity. This is where you will rediscover love, the love of pure spirit.

Meditation is a great solution for people with low self-esteem and for people who haven't learned to love and accept themselves mentally or physically. Meditation can take you on a beautiful journey that will help you to live your life on your terms. It will take you out of your comfort zone and allow you to grow every single day while it reinforces only the good messages you put into your subconscious while you meditate.

Be aware that some painful memories may come up at first; see them for what they were and change your perspective of them in your mind. Once you clear up painful memories, your positive changes will grow exponentially. This is where you change what you believe and implant new beliefs.

Practicing meditation every day helps you learn how to listen to your body and control that part of your subconscious mind that's been telling you there's something wrong with you. When you meditate, the focus is on your inner self and not on the environment.

Practice meditation every day for about 5-10 minutes or more if you can as a means of relaxing, learning about yourself and your behaviors, and retraining your subconscious to relay positive messages during your day. In this way, you can enjoy life more and be better able to serve those around you. You will realize that your goals are easily attainable through focused concentration and you will be able to see that each task within your plan is simply part of who you were meant to be. You will learn to love your path.

"Practice means to perform, over and over again in the face of all obstacles, some act of vision, of faith, of desire. Practice is a means of inviting the perfection desired." (Martha Graham)

In any form of meditation, a sound mantra is used to connect with the higher self. Say this mantra 3 times before you begin your focus preparation, visualization, or breathing exercises to invite the divine energy of the universe into your practice.

Ong (Om) Namo Guru DevNamo

- Ong or Om is the infinite creative energy. Pull in the naval and vibrate the ng or m sound at the root of the nose.

- Namo (nah moe) has the same root as namaste, "reverent greetings" or "I bow to you". Together, ongnamo means "I call on the Infinite Creative Consciousness".

- Guru (gu-dark, ru-light) is the embodiment of wisdom. The first syllable is short and the second long. The r is rolled off the roof of the mouth.

- Dev (dave) means transparent or non-physical.

- Together, these words translate as "I call on the divine teacher or universal wisdom".

Binaural Beats

If you prefer to use binaural beats, you can purchase a Binaural Beats from Amazon or any number of online stores. Or at john-diggs.com/mystore Use them as instructed, with headphones.

The findings of a 2018 study[31,32] suggest that listening to binaural beats for a recommended period can affect a person's subsequent behavior and sleep cycles.

The study authors explain that there are five different categories of frequency pattern:

- **Delta pattern:** Binaural beats in the delta pattern operate at a frequency of 0.5–4 Hz with links to a dreamless sleep. In the study, people who received a delta pattern frequency during sleep entered a deeper stage of sleep, according to electroencephalogram (EEG) brain scan results.

- **Theta pattern:** Practitioners set binaural beats in the theta pattern to a frequency of 4–7 Hz. Theta patterns contribute to improved meditation, creativity, and sleep in the rapid eye movement (REM) phase.

- **Alpha pattern:** Binaural beats in the alpha pattern are at a frequency of 7–13 Hz and may encourage relaxation.

- **Beta pattern:** Binaural beats in the beta pattern are at a frequency of 13–30 Hz. This frequency range may help promote concentration and alertness. However, it can also increase anxiety at the higher end of the range.

- **Gamma pattern:** This frequency pattern accounts for a range of 30–50 Hz. The study authors suggest that these frequencies promote maintenance of arousal while a person is awake.

Don't be alarmed. They won't be what you might expect. These are tones or sound frequencies, a form of sound wave therapy.

APPENDIX III:
GUIDED VISUALIZATION

Visualization is simply the formation of a mental image. It can be an image of an object that is not present or does not yet exist, or it can be a moving image of an event or situation. We can visualize anything that our imagination can produce.

In this guided exercise, you'll learn to imagine a simple food, an apple. You will then go on to visualize that apple with more complexity. You will then add movement and more details as explained in this sample.

You can do this over and over, using different foods or objects until you can effectively visualize complex situations and make them seem real to your subconscious mind. That is the ultimate goal of this exercise. You want to get to the point where your subconscious mind "trusts" these realities, so when you begin to visualize your new life, the way you want it to be, it will trust that this is a reality, that this is really happening.

You'll use concentration and breathing techniques to relax and let go of your conscious self, moving into the subconscious mind and letting it take over. Your goals are to be able to create complete scenarios that are in alignment with what you want to achieve or create. (It's important to first gain a good understanding of the breathing techniques provided in Appendix I.)

In this 4-step process, you will learn to intentionally focus your mind. These exercises are designed to help you learn to use your imagination to create an alternate reality and prepare you for new states of consciousness. Your mind will not know that this is a virtual experience. It will register the experience as having actually happened.

Overview: Step 1: This step is based on certain concentration techniques that will enable you to understand how to focus on what it is you wish to achieve. You will learn to become adept at seeing details in your mind and creating an "experience" that your mind will accept as being real.

Overview: Step 2: This step includes more complex visual creation and movement that will teach you to focus further on what you want to achieve or create.

Overview: Step 3: This step adds more intensity to your vision by adding more objects, building on your ability to create images that are not present in your physical surroundings.

Overview: Step 4: The fourth step is the bridge that will allow you to make an actual passage from visualization to action. You will envision what you want to achieve and allow all the loving energy that surrounds you to edify your strength and spirit in collective cultivation.

Each step in the 4-part process is a threshold for the next step and is important both as a singular step and as part of the group. Incorporating all the attributes of the previous step into the next will strengthen each one.

Setting Your Environment

The space you choose to practice will be considered your Sacred Space. You can practice visualization anywhere, but in the beginning, it's best to create a space where you'll be completely undisturbed. Once you've mastered how to do this, you can be more lenient on where you choose to visualize.

- Choose a quiet space that's out of the way or out of the path of family members, one in which you won't be disturbed. Add some simple meaningful decorations such as candles. This creates an atmosphere of focus and blessing.

- If possible, reserve this space just for the purpose of practicing your guided visualization. The space should have a fresh feeling and a moderate temperature, not too hot or cold and without drafts. The floor should be padded or carpeted, or you can use a comfortable thick mat.

- If you're practicing on a hard wood floor or outdoors on the ground, put something between you and the floor. This will keep the Earth's magnetic field from draining your energy.

- As your body goes into deep relaxation, it will naturally begin to cool off. Keep a light blanket handy for deep relaxation.

- It's best to wear comfortable clothing that does not constrict. If possible, wear white, the color of the Infinite, and cover your head with a natural fiber cloth to enhance the meditative mind and strengthen your electromagnetic field.

Remember, you have unlimited capacity. While practicing the 3-step program, use these keys to help you access your gift.

"Nature does not hurry yet everything is accomplished."

- Lao Tzu

- **Be positive.** Think about the beneficial aspects of transforming your life so you can Love Life to the fullest rather than the debilitating aspects of negativity. What the mind has created it can also un-create or recreate.

- **Fix your mind.** Think about anything that's good or lovely, such as a child you care about, a memorable trip or something special someone did for you. Avoid painful memories even if they involve loved ones. Painful memories require emotional healing, something you may choose to do once you've mastered the basics of visualization.

- **Be specific.** In the same way you might give orders to a corporate team or a child who needs guidance, you will create boundaries for your intention, such as "I will now be shown how to gain better health" or "I will now be shown the obstacles that prevent me from getting a raise."

- **Learn as you go.** Once you begin and as you progress, you'll find yourself able to hone in on more detailed needs. Begin with small things.

- **Take your time.** You'll need time to unwind and get in the zone, so don't be in a hurry. Your answers may indeed come right away, but they won't come at all if your mind, body, and spirit are not in a state of relaxation.

How to Perform Each Step

Take about 10 minutes for each session. You should strive for a neutral state of mind, clearing your thoughts and keeping your mind empty of any distractions. Your objective is to become a blank canvas that you will fill with your intention for a new subconscious experience. When you're finished with each session, drink water to balance and ground yourself.

You have already prepared a space which is clean, comfortable and decorated with things that make you feel happy and peaceful. Your Sacred Space is a place of love which you have created and in which you will practice undisturbed. Here you will learn to experience a union of Spirit with ego or self. Only in this union can you connect to the power within you.

Before starting each session, you will:

1. **Relax your body.** Take a position of relaxation, one in which your neck, arms and legs are comfortable and your breathing is not constricted. You can sit or lie down, but it's recommended that you don't lie on a bed. You want to associate a neutral position and place with the practice, not one in which you sleep in every night. This way the practice is not associated with sleep but with waking mindfulness.

2. **Empty all thoughts from your mind.** Sit or lie in your Sacred Space and draw in the peace and harmony in the room. You may hear some distant noise from outside. This is normal and often inevitable. Ignore it and continue clearing your mind. Your position is otherwise unimportant, as long as you are comfortable.

3. **Close your eyes.**

Practice Objective

Your objective in this practice is to learn to visualize in detail an object and surroundings that are not physically present. Each step will continue for 7 days.

Step 1: Do this for 7 days.

Choose an apple or some other simple food item and imagine what it looks like. Try to assimilate every detail of the food and how you envision the surroundings in which it's located. Create and take in as much detail as possible.

Imagine you are eating an apple. Don't think about calories or dietary restrictions that may be part of your daily life. Simply envision the food and all the details that might surround it. Make it a moving vision, not a static one.

Don't just see an apple sitting in a bowl. Hold it and turn it over in your hand. Look at every detail, such as the color and variations in the skin tone, the stem, the leaves, the possible bruises. Is it a large apple or a small crabapple? Is it red or green? Create as many details as you can using all your submodalities.

Step 2: Do this for 7 days.

Repeat the same action as in Step 1, but with just one added ingredient. Perhaps it will be a baked apple with whipped cream on top.

You can repeat the entire process of seeing the apple or you can begin with creating the vision using the new ingredient.

Your food is visible to you. What kind of dish is it on? Can you see the juice from the apple under the whipped cream? How high is the whipped cream? Is it in a swirling pile on top of the apple or does it run around the perimeter of the plate in a decorative row? Remember to create and see as many details as possible.

Step 3: Do this for 7 days.

Repeat the same action as Step 2, only this time you will add a beverage.

You will see the colors, bubbles, glass and so on. Is the glass full or only partly filled? Is it even in a glass? Perhaps it's in a bottle. What color is the bottle? Is it glass or plastic? Does it have a cork, a lid or a twist top? Feel it in your hand. Is it warm or cold?

Step 4: Do this for 7 days.

Repeat Step 3, but now you will actually see yourself eating that food and drinking that beverage. Remember to create and see as much detail as possible. On this day, you will take stock of what you're experiencing, not just what you're seeing.

You will use all your senses and submodalities to remember the entire experience.

- **Sight** - See every detail as you've been doing. Has the skin turned brown from baking? Is the cream melted or did you put it on after the bake?

- **Sound** - This is a powerful visionary tool. You will try to hear yourself laughing when you bite into the apple. Listen for the crunch it makes.

- **Taste** - The apple will be sweet or tart, perhaps spicy. What are you getting in terms of taste? Remember, this is your creation.

- **Smell** - You can actually smell an apple's fragrance. Try to imagine what it smells like.

- **Touch** - Is the apple's skin slick? It's wet and juicy inside. Can you feel the juice running down your face? What is the mouth-feel?

Never rush through this exercise. In doing so, you will miss the details that are so important to honing your ability to visualize. Incorporate each of the senses into your vision, so as you're seeing the apple, you also taste it, smell it, feel its shiny skin, and hear the sounds you make as you eat it.

Here's an example of a highly detailed vision in which we will continue to use an apple as our food. Keeping your vision simple in the beginning will teach you to focus on minute details, so complexity is not your objective. This example is merely to demonstrate how details can make an image more vivid. Once you've mastered the art of simple visualization, you can work your way up to more detailed images that are in alignment with what you want for your life.

Picture that apple's beginnings. See yourself in the orchard, walking around, looking at the trees for the perfect apple. Then see yourself climbing the tree, perhaps using a ladder or with the help of a friend, picking the apple and shining it on your shirtsleeve.

Look at the variations in the skin color. Is the apple a deep crimson or does it have russet and green striations? Did you manage to capture a leaf or two when you plucked it from the branch?

Now smell the apple. See yourself holding it up to your nose and think about the fragrant fresh-picked aroma that only an apple can give. Perhaps you've given visual presence to the aroma in the form of an imaginary wisp.

Now take a bite of the apple and taste the juicy sweet or tart flesh. Hear the crunch as your teeth break into the fruit's skin and see yourself laughing as the juice runs down your chin. If you can, add sound to your vision.

In your vision, your eyes are open as you take another bite. Sit on the ground and feel the crisp fresh air that permeates a sunny fall day. You are happy and content, sitting there eating your apple. Listen to the leaves rustling around you in the breeze. Maybe there are children playing in the leaves. Watch them tumble around and hear them giggle.

What does the sky look like? Is it bright and sunny, are there a few wispy clouds floating by? Is there a farm stand or other people moving about? Placing movement into your vision will make it more real to your mind.

Now you're getting ready to prepare your apple dessert. You're moving around doing all the ordinary things that you do in your kitchen. See the colors, the utensils on the counter and the refrigerator door open and close as you watch yourself get the ingredients from inside it. Maybe you even hear the refrigerator motor kick on.

Watch yourself gather all the ingredients you need such as butter, flour, your apple, cinnamon, a cutting board, and knife. Go through all the motions in your mind that you would need to go through to make this apple dessert. Did you hear the pan clatter as you removed it from the cupboard? Did you spill some flour or spice on the counter? See it. Wipe it up. Make it real.

Perhaps you need to turn on the oven and set the timer. When the timer goes off, open the oven door and smell the delicate aroma of apples, butter and cinnamon. See the steam coming from the pan. Put on hot mitts, remove the pan from the oven and set it on the table. Hear the oven door close. Did the pan make a sound when you placed it on the cooling rack?

Would you like ice cream on top? Did the kids come into the kitchen wanting some of your dessert, laughing and pleading for you to give them some?

Sit down and pour your beverage. Cut into the dessert or spoon it into a dish and taste it, allowing yourself to savor the complex tastes that you've assembled. Will you hear the pop of a cork, the sound of the fizz and the tune of liquid pouring into the glass? You will feel the hot or cool liquid as it touches your lips and taste it as it enters your mouth. Is it sweet or tart, warm or cold? These are all details you must conjure down to the smallest bit in order to produce a realistic image that you have crafted and which you control.

In a successful vision, you will have sensed your body. You will have been mindful of details such as plates, glasses, silverware, your kitchen or table and chairs, and each and every movement that was made. Time will have appeared to slow down. Everything should have appeared to move in slow motion as you reached for the food, brought it to your mouth, and chewed.

Now you will focus on how you felt after the actual eating experience and try to mirror the same level of satisfaction that your vision brought.

Feel free to smile, relax further, or laugh. Congratulate yourself for this great accomplishment. This was your creation, something you took control of. Remember that your imagination brought that vision and those sensations to you. Your ability to create the enjoyment of actually eating that food will be associated with your ability to conjure something from nothing.

As far as your mind is concerned, it will simply remember this as a real experience. Your mind doesn't know that this didn't physically happen. You've created a trust in your own ability so that the next time you try to create something from nothing, your mind will remember that trust as you begin to focus your thoughts on regenesis. You can experience the creation process by simply imagining it in the same way you did with the apple.

ACKNOWLEDGEMENTS

I would like to sincerely thank all my family, my friends, my mentors and role models for their many years of unconditional love and unwavering support. I am who I am because of you and I am sincerely BlessednGrateful for it! Thank you very much for Loving me and for making it easier for me to Love Life!

I must also sincerely Thank Ms. Lee Caleca for her editing expertise, her tireless research and for her inspiring dedication to all my *Can You DIGG It?* ™ Books!.

ABOUT THE AUTHOR

John Diggs is a Certified Life Coach, Certified NLP Practitioner, and Mind Mapping Master. He lives with his wife and daughters in Val Vista Lakes, Arizona. You can contact him at john@JohnDiggs.com

REFERENCES

1. Anapol, Deborah, Ph.D. "What Is Love, and What Isn't?" Psychology Today, Nov. 2011 https://www.psychologytoday.com/us/blog/love-without-limits/201111/what-is-love-and-what-isnt

2. Merline, Dr. Galina. "The Human Body Frequency." Heal Tone. 2015 https://www.healtone.com/pages/the-human-body-frequency.html

3. Samuels, Ron. "The Healing Effect of Sound Frequency." Heal Tone. 2015 https://www.healtone.com/pages/The-Healing-Effect-of-Sound-Frequency.html

4. Staff. "What is Frequency and Why You Need to Know About it." thesoulfrequency, 2020 https://thesoulfrequency.com/frequency/

5. Staff. "528Hz Sound "Miraculously" Cleaned Oil, Polluted Water in the Gulf of Mexico, According to a New Study by a Canadian Researcher." I528Tunes Netplay https://www.528records.com/pages/528hz-sound-miraculously-cleaned-oil-polluted-water-gulf-mexico-according-new-study-canadian-r

6. Zimmerman, Jacquelyn W. et al. "Targeted treatment of cancer with radiofrequency electromagnetic fields amplitude-modulated at tumor-specific frequencies." Chinese Journal of Cancer, U.S. National Library of Medicine,

Nov. 2013 https://www.ncbi.nlm.nih.gov/pmc/articles/
PMC3845545/

7. Lynes, Barry. The Cancer Cure That Worked! Fifty Years
    of Suppression. Lake Tahoe, CA: BioMed Publishing
    Group, 1987

8. Vey, Gary. "The 432 vs 440 Controversy." Viewzone. 2014
    http://www.viewzone.com/432hertz222.html

9. Gonzalez, Andrew, M.D, J.D., MPH. "What are binau-
    ral beats, and how do they work?" Medical News Today.
    Healthline Media, Sept. 2019 https://www.medicalnewsto-
    day.com/articles/320019#how-do-binaural-beats-work

10. Tu, Chau. "Seeing the Patterns in Sound." Science
    Friday, Nov, 2016 https://www.sciencefriday.com/articles/
    seeing-the-patterns-in-sound/

11. Staff. "Dr. Masaru Emoto and Water Consciousness." The
    Wellness Enterprise. 2016 https://thewellnessenterprise.
    com/emoto/

12. Nhat Hanh, Thich. "Fear & Fearlessness: Essential Wisdom
    for Getting Through the Storm." Watkins Mind Body Spirit.
    Issue 32: 2012-2013

13. McKie, Robin. "What makes Us? Nature or nurture? The
    DNA debate comes back to life." The Guardian. 2020
    https://www.theguardian.com/science/2018/nov/11/
    nature-or-nurture-debate-three-identical-strangers-film

14. Buss, DM. "The great struggles of life: Darwin and the emer-
    gence of evolutionary psychology." American Psychology.
    PubMed.gov. U.S. National Library of Medicine, Feb. 2009
    https://www.ncbi.nlm.nih.gov/pubmed/19203146

15. Lipton, Bruce H. Ph.D. The Biology of Belief: Unleashing the Power of Consciousness, Matter & Miracles. New York: Hay House, 2015

16. Gholipour, Bahar. "From the Deepest Coma, New Brain Activity Found." Live Science. Future US Inc, Sept. 2013 https://www.livescience.com/39761-brain-activity-deep-coma.html

17. Robbins, Tony. "We ALL have an IDENTITY..." Posts. Facebook, April 8, 2019 https://www.facebook.com/TonyRobbins/posts/we-all-have-an-identity-a-set-of-beliefs-that-define-who-we-are-what-we-can-and-/10157363007479060/

18. Brown, Joel. "Tony Robbins 6 Key Principles For Finding Your True Identity." Addicted to Success. July 2013 https://addicted2success.com/success-advice/tony-robbins-6-key-principles-for-finding-your-true-identity/

19. Buzan, Tony. Mind Map Mastery: The Complete Guide to Learning and Using the Most Powerful Thinking Tool in the Universe. London: Watkins Media Limited, 2018

20. Osimo, Sofia Adelaide, et al. "Conversations between self and self as Sigmund Freud-A firtual body ownership paradigm for self-counselling." Nature Scientific Reports. Nature Research/Springer Nature, Sept. 2015 https://www.nature.com/articles/srep13899

21. Antanaityte, Neringa. "How to effortlessly have more positive thoughts." Mind Matters. Tlex Institute. Accessed April 14, 2020 https://tlexinstitute.com/how-to-effortlessly-have-more-positive-thoughts/4910/

22. Grinder, John and Bostic St. Clair, Carmen. https://www.johngrinder.com/

23. Beale, Michael. "NLP Technique: Senses and Submodalities." Nlp-techniques.org. NLP Techniques, 2020 https://www.nlp-techniques.org/what-is-nlp/senses-submodalities/

24. Ebling, Paul. The "Marshmallow Test" and Your Mind." HeffX. Live Trading News, Oct. 2017 https://www.livetradingnews.com/marshmallow-test-mind-58077.html#.XnehhYhKiUn

25. Staff. "Imagineering." Wikipedia. Wikipedia Creative Commons, March 2020. Archived from the original. "The Place They Do Imagineering". Time. p. 59 Feb. 1942

26. George, Selvin, Evans, David, Davidson, Lance. "A Biologically Inspired Programming Model for Self-Healing Systems." University of Virginia. National Science Foundation and NASA Langley Research Center 2002 http://www.cs.virginia.edu/~evans/pubs/woss.pdf

27. Rein, Glen Ph.D. Proceeds of the International Forum on New Science. Effect of Conscious Intention on Human DNA. 1996. http://item-bioenergy.com/infocenter/consciousintentiononDNA.pdf

28. Akin, Maxwell. "Neville Goddard's Method for Creating Reality." M. Medium, May 2018 https://medium.com/@maxwellakin/neville-goddards-method-for-creating-reality-556d9354f559

29. Sicinski, Adam. "Here's Why You Need to Take Massive Action to Achieve Your Goals." IQ Matrix. Accessed April 3, 2020 https://blog.iqmatrix.com/massive-action

30. Hicks, Esther and Hicks, Jerry. Ask and It is Given: Learning to Manifest Your Desires. P. 114. Carlsbad, CA: Hay House, Inc. 2004

31. Smith, Lori, BSN, MSN, CRNP. "What are binaural beats, and how do they work?" Medical News Today. Healthline Media, Sept. 2019 https://www.medicalnewstoday.com/articles/320019

32. Padmanabhan, R., Hildreth, A.J., and Laws, D. "A prospective, randomised, controlled study examining binaural beat audio and pre-operative anxiety in patients undergoing general anaesthesia for day case surgery." Wiley Online Library. Anesthesia Vol 60 Issue 9, July 2005 https://onlinelibrary.wiley.com/doi/full/10.1111/j.1365-2044.2005.04287.x

Other Books by John Diggs

I AM – A Dynamic Look at How Re-Anchoring Your Beliefs and Identity Can Free Your Life for Excellent Health, Extraordinary Wealth, Enormous Success, and Extreme Happiness

BlessednGrateful – Discover the Secret to Loving Life Right Now!

DIGG This Too! – 4 more Can You DIGG It Powers to help you Love Life Deeper

Big Play Power – How to make Big Plays in and out of Sports to Love Life

I AM The Game – How to Master The Game within The Game to Love The Game

Made in United States
Orlando, FL
22 March 2026

79558358R00125